Design Your Own Website With WordPress

The ultimate, step-by-step, beginner's guide to a full-featured WordPress website for small business, coaches, authors & bloggers

NO CODING REQUIRED | SAVE EXPENSIVE DESIGNER FEES

NARAYAN KUMAR

www.designWPsite.com

Table of Contents

1. Here's a map of your journey

Welcome to your own website! And here we are at the very start of the build.

Today is reading day. You take it all in. You learn all the background stuff you need to know for a good grasp of the fundamentals.

Before you know it, you will be diving into the deep end. With my friendly guiding hand on your shoulder.

What kind of a book is this? Does it tell you everything?

This is a hands-on guide to teach you skills that will save you big, fat designer/developer fees. It is a practical guide to website building, not a theoretical textbook.

Keep the guide open and execute the steps on your computer (not phone or tablet but on a desktop or laptop.) By the end of the book, you will have built a fully functional, secure, and feature-rich business website.

This is a practical, to-do book. Treat me as you would a friend who is good at something. I will lay a friendly hand on your shoulder and tell you only what's necessary. I will say, "Do this and then do this" and keep moving you along rather than stop at every little step and tell you every back story.

I think it's more natural to learn a new tool this way. To learn Powerpoint, for instance, you wouldn't painfully go through explanations of every menu item and sub-menu item in the app before making a single slide!

Yet I've seen beginner tutorials on PowerPoint that explain obscure little details without an overall context.

Our tool of choice for building a website is WordPress, a free (but complex) piece of software. It can do a thousand things, for sure. Does that mean you have to learn all the thousand things before you can build your website? No way.

We have all visited countless websites. So we already know what a website should be all about. No rocket science there. We will apply this common sense awareness to arrive at a goal we are happy to reach.

Learning something new always feels strange. Once you get past that feeling, learning becomes pretty simple.

You don't need any prior knowledge of how websites are built to use this book. You probably know next to nothing about WordPress, the free software we will be using to build our site. It does not matter. And you certainly don't need any knowledge about coding and tech stuff.

WordPress builds websites. It's the world's most popular software for doing that. Once you have a working knowledge of WordPress you can easily build a website for yourself (or someone else) with whatever features you have in mind.

Who is this book for?

This book teaches you **how to make a website for a small business or a personal blog.** It is a step-by-step guide that you can personalize for your needs easily.

If you are any of the following, this book can help you in a practical and relevant manner.

- Consultant
- Yoga trainer
- Executive Coach
- Life coach
- Holistic medicine practitioner
- Therapist
- Blogger, writer or author
- Designer or copywriter looking to expand their skillset
- Landscaping service provider
- Plumber
- Dentist
- Financial Advisor
- Any professional who offers an online service through time slots
- A small business owner

You get the idea. **As long as yours is a small business and you are not selling products online**, this book is a perfect fit for you.

To be clear, this book is not for e-commerce businesses that sell products or services for money straight off the site. (What you will learn here are all the necessary steps for building *any kind of website*. It's just that an e-commerce site is an advanced, complex application that requires additional steps than are covered in this guide.)

Why build a website? Isn't social media good enough?

Since you purchased this book, you probably already know the value of a website. But let's discuss the key aspects quickly.

Social media content is a stream – a constantly changing landscape of fresh content replacing old content... of a few minutes ago! Beyond catching visitors in some random fashion, you aren't assured of the consistent exposure of your message. If you need consistent exposure, then you have to have paid ads on social media.

Are paid ads effective for your line of business? It is a debatable subject, but the costs are real and recurring. Difficult to sustain for small businesses, professionals, and bloggers.

Further, the content on any social media platform belongs to them, not you. If you publish something 'improper', the platform may even decide to ban you. Your content disappears, you cease to exist there. You don't own anything on social media including all the original stuff you put up there. Let's be clear on that.

On the other hand, **your website is your website from day one** and forever. Your content remains steady and visible to whoever visits, not a scrolling stream.

The best combination for building your brand is to **use streaming, transient social media to drive traffic to your permanent, stable web pages.** This can be powerful as thousands of businesses have discovered.

Why use WordPress to build? Why not Wix or Squarespace?

You may have heard of template sites like Wix or Weebly or Squarespace. They offer you a ready space for your website on the internet and also some ready-made templates.

Targeted at non-coders and novices, these sites give you pre-designed web pages from which you choose the ones you fancy. You replace the sample content with your own (text, visuals, etc.), and - voila! - your website is ready.

You pay a monthly subscription. You don't need to know any tech stuff. These sites are easy to use for anyone looking for a quick and dirty solution for their business website.

There is nothing wrong with using such websites. But be aware of the limitations. Being template-based, you can choose the closest template that fits your business. But that's about it. Sooner or later, you'll find it's not quite the perfect fit it promised to be.

Besides, as with social media platforms, the content you create here will vanish the moment the company decides to leave the game. That may or may not happen, but who can guarantee that?

As some of my clients discovered (and then became my clients), you are truly 'stuck' with template-based sites. If you outgrow the template there is no easy way to transfer your site elsewhere. You are locked in.

Finally, there is the monthly charge you keep dishing out.

By contrast, a WordPress site is based on free software. Barring a yearly spend on your domain name and domain hosting subscriptions, you pay nothing to anyone.

(We'll get into domain name and domain hosting in the next chapter.)

A WordPress site gives you ownership from day one. If you want to leave the game someday, it will be your call. No one else's.

It's easy to learn too. If you can do a slide presentation using software like PowerPoint, you can build a website using WordPress.

Obviously, the functionalities are more extensive and complex than slide presentation software, but they are not difficult to learn.

You are holding a book in your hands that promises a full website build starting from scratch with no prior knowledge. That in itself should tell you how doable this is.

Put aside an hour or two every day to learn the steps. And you'll have something built by your own hands for your own use with your own content talking to your own audience. In about two weeks.

Let's dive in.

What kind of a site are we building here?

We will be building a website for a career coach, who has online clients. We will pretend (at first) that you are the career coach and create a website accordingly. We will build a 5-page website that includes the following:

- A content-rich **Home** page (front page)
- An **About** page that talks about the coach's expertise
- A **Contact** page so people can reach the coach
- A **Services** page that displays the business offerings
- A **Blog** page to share the coach's professional suggestions and tips
- Along with a **common header** at the top of each page (including the navigation menu) and a **common footer** at the bottom of each page

We will have a solid, fully functional website at the end of it.

And, yes, I hear you say, but I'm not a career coach! Why am I building a career coach's website if I'm not one? What if I'm a plumber or landscaper? What if I'm a blogger? What if I'm something else? Isn't it a waste of time and energy to be building something other than what I need?

Hold on to your horses. Here are TWO practical approaches I recommend you consider and choose one of them, right at the start of the journey (and stick with it).

Approach 1: Build a career coach's website exactly as described in the book, whether you are a career coach or not. All the text you need will be provided by me, so you don't have to write anything. With the knowledge gained, **you will know enough by the end of Chapter 9 to create a custom website for your business.** Just tweak the content and design already there. Add new features that your business needs. Delete stuff that your business doesn't need. (You'll know how to do all that by the time you reach that point.)

Approach 2: This is tricky but some of you may find it easier to do. And that is to use your own text and images from the very beginning. As you learn the ropes of building every page, you keep supplying your own design choices, color choices, relevant text, videos, images, and everything else. So by Chapter 9 you pretty much have your unique website built and ready to launch.

Approach 1 is what I strongly recommend. Especially if you're new to WordPress, you will learn WordPress without getting sidetracked by content and design choices. Plus if you lose your way it will be difficult to catch up because my screen displays will be different from yours.

Note: If the idea here is to use a career coach's website as a template that you can tweak, then, hey, isn't that the same idea behind template sites like Wix? No, not really. The difference is that the template you choose from a site like Wix is the one you use finally with whatever features it has; whereas the career coach template in this book is the starting point **to learn to build whatever site you want.** It's the difference between getting a ready-made sketch that you color in and learning how to draw different things.

Once you've built all the pages with my guidance, you will know how to:

- build **pages**
- design **sections** within pages
- drag and drop **elements** (text, images, etc.) within sections
- **edit and revise** anything

That's the whole point of the book - teaching you how to custom-build with WordPress (along with a theming plugin called **Elementor**, but we'll get to that shortly.)

With this skill, **you can revisit the completed career coach website after Chapter 9 and reshape it into whatever you want.** You can add and delete stuff on every page depending on what matters to you. You can write and rewrite your copy as many times as you wish to get it perfect.

You can search for the perfect images that should feature on your website. You can browse YouTube for the perfect videos that serve your purpose.

You can change fonts and re-design layouts the way you wish.

It will all fall into place, I assure you. Especially when you also have at your disposal a collection of **voice-free videos on my site that I call SilentMoves to follow all the mouse clicks and moves** mentioned in the book.

There are as many as 27 SilentMoves videos, brief and to the point, to help you complete the different tasks in the book. Taken with the text and the copious screenshots, you will have all the tools at hand to learn everything. Let's get hands-on then!

Note: The next chapter, you should know, has less to do with WordPress and more to do with a couple of preliminary steps. You are planting your very own flag in the internet landscape - in the form of your domain name and your domain hosting. Without these, you can't build your WordPress site. The upcoming chapter will probably be the most technical chapter in the entire book. The rest is a breeze.

◆◆◆

2. Domain name & domain hosting

L et's start with the first step of getting a domain name for your website. As mentioned, this is a name of your choice and has nothing to do with WordPress itself.

You're going to come up with a name for your business website. Exciting! Even if you're a hobbyist learning about WordPress, you still need a name for your website. You can't build a website without a domain name.

So decide on a name. It could be as simple as taking your business name and making it into your domain name.

How to choose your site name

Important Note: For this step, **choose a real name for your rea** **business**, not the career coach we're pretending to be. Because your rea website is what this website is going to be eventually.

For example, if you have a plumbing service called Joe Blackburn Plumbing it can easily become your domain name by 'crushing' it al together: joeblackburnplumbing.com. (You can't have spaces in a domain name, unfortunately.)

Be easy to remember and relevant. Don't use hyphens in your domain name, though. Hyphens make it difficult for people to type in. For visual clarity you can use a mix of capital and lower case letters to separate the words: JoeBlackburnPlumbing.com

That makes for easier reading by humans. The internet doesn't care one way or the other.

The point is even if your visitor forgets to type the capitalization in the exact places you intended or forgets to use capital letters totally, they will still reach your site. Provided the overall spelling is correct, of course.

You may not want a domain name that mimics your business name. That's fine too. You may have options on the table such as:

plumbingforless.com

plumbexpress.com

yourlocalplumber.com

topplumbinginmiami.com

And so on. You get the picture. It's totally up to you to decide the kind of name you want for your website. Brainstorm with your spouse, colleague, or friend.

Once you have a domain name you have to purchase it and also **get it registered with a domain name registrar** so that the internet will then recognize it and treat it as a valid address. It is a one-step process, really. You purchase it, it gets registered automatically.

Before we proceed any further though, we should check if a website with your chosen name already exists. That happens fairly often, by the way.

To check if your domain name is already taken, go to **domaintools.whois.com** and enter your domain name in the box and click on the 'Search' button. If you get a green box with 'yoursitename.com is for sale' you're good to go. If you get the detailed record of a website instead, it means a website by that name already exists and the name is taken.

Once you know it's available, you can purchase your domain name. Once you purchase it, it is automatically registered. From where do you purchase a domain name? From the same place you will purchase your domain hosting. Let's head there.

Get yourself some domain hosting (and a domain name)

Let's go to a trusted and popular web hosting company like Bluehost.com. Click on this link: https://bit.ly/3L4D25d

(It's my affiliate link and I get paid a commission. You pay the same price whether you go to Bluehost directly or through the link above.)

The page you see will depend on what promo offer the company is running at this time. Generally, you will see a 'Get Started' or similar button to click on. I want you to consider the two cheapest options (with a good promotional offer, if you're lucky) and choose one of them.

The **Basic Plan** allows a single website to be built. It is good enough for our purposes. Rest assured you can build the website in this book without any compromise if you go with this plan.

The **Plus Plan** allows you to host unlimited websites. Is that a good thing when all you're building is a single site? Well, once you learn the ropes in the coming days, you may feel like developing a WordPress site for your spouse's gardening hobby or a friend's blog on racing bikes, or your daughter's photo gallery or you may want a second site for your side hustle... you get the picture. You may even want to build a site for a stranger and earn a fee.

Decide on your hosting plan and the screen will bring up a choice between creating a new domain and using your own domain. Fill in the box on the left ('Create a new domain name') with the domain name   you decided on earlier. See screenshot below.

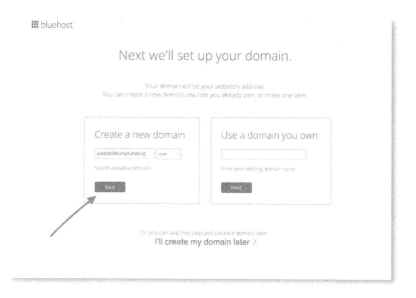

Click on the 'Next' button. You will see the **Account Information** page. Fill in your name, phone, email, etc.

In the Package Information section, choose the duration – 1 year or more, whichever you wish. Below that, you will see a list of items to buy under 'Package Extras'. **You don't need any of these. Untick all of them.**

Note: The **Bluehost charges are annual,** not outright. Like every web hosting company out there, Bluehost too offers a ridiculously low fee for the first year to hook you in. But it steeply escalates from the second year onwards to a 'regular rate'.

Use the Payment Information down the page to purchase. Congratulations! You have purchased domain hosting plus a domain name for your business.

Installing WordPress

The site will instruct you to create your account in Bluehost. Great idea. It's a useful thing to know how to get in and get out of Bluehost. Click on the blue 'Create your account' button.

On the 'Create Your New Password' page type in your password twice and click on 'Create Account'. You will see the message "Your account is ready to go...' with a blue button saying 'Go to login.' Click on the button and on the next screen enter your password and click on the 'Login' button.

A new page promising the beginning of an adventure comes along and you click the 'Create your website' button. In the next 3 screens, look for the 'Skip this step' at the very bottom and click on it each time (no harm if you fill in stuff here, but it's not necessary and you get to save some time.) You will come to the screen shown above.

Take the option on the left: 'Limitless customization' and click on the 'Get started' button below. You are about to install WordPress software.

The screen now says, 'Let's create a website'. That is another way of saying 'Let Bluehost install WordPress for you in this empty wasteland you have purchased.'

What is displayed on this page and the following 3 pages is unnecessary from our point of view, but there is no way to stop it. In these pages, Bluehost tries to figure out how it can create the 'perfect' WordPress site for you. But we don't need that. We're going to build our very own customization instead.

So, on this page and the next 3 pages, I encourage you to click on the 'Skip this step' link at the bottom. Don't worry, it'll make our work easier.

Bluehost will get to work and install WordPress. A message on the screen will pop up: "Great work! We're installing WordPress..."

When it's done in a few minutes, we get to the Welcome page. It means that your copy of WordPress has been installed for your exclusive use on Bluehost. Click on the button 'Log into WordPress' (top right of the screen.)

You are now looking at your WordPress site - although with a lot of confusing information everywhere (see screenshot above). We will clean it all up soon. But for now, breathe! Oh, joyous day! Here's your new website!

You have installed WordPress on your domain host with your domain name. Once we clean it all up and perform some basic housekeeping, we will be ready to build our site as we please.

Get WordPress ready for your visits

You already have a username and password to enter the Bluehost site. It's from there that you entered your WordPress site seamlessly without the need for another password for the WordPress site.

This is not ideal. Because when you want to edit your WordPress site, you'll have to first log in to your Bluehost account and from there get into your site using the same 'Log into WordPress' button we clicked on moments ago. Painful. And easily avoidable too.

We want to access our WordPress site directly without going via Bluehost every time. To do this we establish a unique set of credentials (username and password) for our WordPress site. Scan the narrow black column on the left, which lists several items.

In the left column click on **Users**. Right now there is only a single authorized user on this site - and that's you. Hover your mouse over your username and you will see 'Edit | View' links under it. Click on Edit. Scroll down midway and fill in your first name, last name, and nickname. Notice that the username is greyed out, so you can't change it. Check that your email is correct.

Set a new password of your choice by clicking the 'Set New Password' button near the bottom of the page. Go all the way down and click on the blue 'Update Profile' button. Your settings will be saved and the same page will refresh itself. Note down the username and password somewhere safe

Not necessary but nice to have

An interesting thing you can get done here on this page - although not strictly necessary - is your **profile photo**. This is not as straightforward as uploading your image.

You'll have to right-click the underlined link (toward the bottom of the page) that says 'You can change your profile picture on Gravatar.' Why right-click? Because it keeps the current tab active and opens up the external site - **gravatar.com** - in a separate tab.

So right-click on that link if you're interested. Since this step is optional (and also very easy to do), I won't get into details. You can follow the simple steps to upload your photo to gravatar.com once you register yourself. Remember to use the same mail id that you used inWordPress.

Once you do the Gravatar bit, go back to the browser tab that has the Users page in WordPress. Refresh the page and you will see your photo staring back at you down the page. This image is used on the website in different places and also gets shown when you go to someone else's WordPress site and comment on their blog post.

Chapter Summary

- You finalized your domain name
- You bought yourself your chosen domain name + domain hosting at bluehost.com
- You had Bluehost install WordPress in your account
- You created your username and password for your WordPress site
- You (optionally) created your Gravatar image
◆ ◆ ◆

3. Getting to know WordPress

We jumped in at the deep end and completed a lot of pre-WordPress work. As well as installing WordPress software itself on your site.

A minor, but important, piece of work remains to be done at Bluehost.com. **Let's make your website an https:// site rather than an http:// site.**

Did you even notice the difference? The addition of an 's' to 'http' makes your site secure, trust me. It's a big deal. No modern site should be insecure.

You have to get this done by getting a **valid SSL certificate** (free) from your hosting company. Once you have it, your site address will start with 'https://' as it should. So head over to bluehost.com and login, if you're not logged in already.

Getting your SSL certificate

Login to bluehost.com using your credentials (you saved them, right?). In the left column click on the 'Advanced' link at the bottom.

Scroll down a bit till you reach the Security section. Click on the 'SSL/TLS Status' link (see screenshot below).

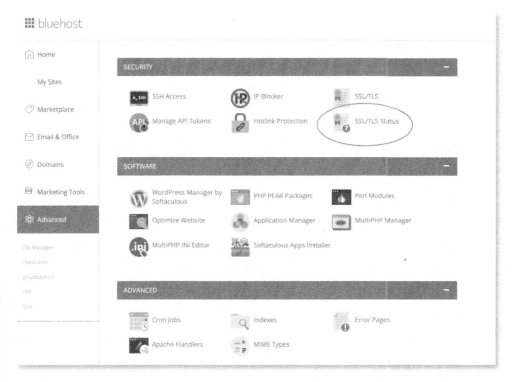

On the SSL/TLS Status page, you will see a listing of various sites that include your domain plus a few variations using prefixes. Select them all by clicking on the checkbox in the left-most column (to the left of the 'Domain' column title).

Now click the blue button that reads 'AutoSSL'. In a few moments, the job is done. Let's get into the exciting world of WordPress now.

Diving into WordPress: Cleaning up the plugins page

Get back to your WordPress site (or log in if you closed all your tabs.) You are at the back end of your website staring at a visually noisy and talkative page. We will clean this up shortly. This is the basic vanilla WordPress, the same as thousands of others upon installation.

If you want to know what the front end of your website looks like, mouse over to the top left of the page, where you see a tiny house icon. Click on it.

There. From the plain vanilla back end of your site, you're now looking at the plain vanilla front end of your site! This is how thousands of brand new, just-installed WordPress sites look like to visitors. Look around. Nothing much to see, right? Let's get back.

Note: The terms 'front-end' and 'back-end' are fancy ways of describing the two views of your website: a *front end* for your visitors to see and navigate and a *back end* exclusively for you to access and manage. The back end view is also known as the **admin view.**

Click on the top left corner of the screen on the site name once more. You'll be back at the back end. Look at the left column in black. About midway down the list, click on **'Plugins'.** You will be taken to a page that lists all the plugins on your site, which are bits of additional software.

How did they get here at all? How did they show up uninvited when all we did was install the basic WordPress software? Who installed these plugins? Bluehost, that's who.

Since *we* get to decide what plugins we need and what we don't, we will now remove these plugins from our site. (We will later add our own, after we learn a little more about plugins.)

Incidentally, deleting these plugins will also have an excellent side-effect: Those talkative, noisy boxes of information that made no sense to you will all vanish.

Tick the checkboxes alongside every plugin like Akismet, Hello Dolly, OptinMonster, etc. **Deleting plugins is a two-step process,** although it takes just seconds. First, you deactivate them, then you delete them. Click on the 'Bulk actions' dropdown menu on top of the list of plugins and choose 'Deactivate'. Click on the 'Apply' button alongside. Say OK to any box that asks you to confirm your choice.

Once deactivated, plugins can be deleted. Tick those checkboxes next to the plugins once again. Click on the 'Bulk actions' dropdown menu and choose 'Delete'. Click on the 'Apply' button. Say yes to the confirmation box. And watch them disappear in front of your eyes.

Great. Click on 'Dashboard' in the black column on the left. It's the topmost item on the list. You will see a busy page again that we will silence right now. Click on the top right where you see the words 'Screen Options'. See circled in the screenshot below. (Your version of WordPress incidentally will say 6.2 or later depending on when you read this.)

On the screen that opens up, uncheck the checkboxes you see. Click on

'Screen Options' again. It's all clean and neat now. Later, when you get to grips with the details of WordPress, you can selectively get back just those information boxes you find useful. For now, clean and

clutter-free is the best way forward.

Diving into WordPress: Basic settings

Look at the left column in black. Isn't the list of items looking suddenly shorter? Yes, it's because we deleted all those plugins, most of which added their own links to the list.

Toward the bottom of the list, hover over the **'Settings'** link. You will see a sub-menu from which you can click on **'General'**. (Or you can click on 'Settings' and you will see a sub-list of items under it, from which you can click on 'General'.)

Our quest to 'non-vanilla-fy' our generic WordPress site begins here. Let's fill in the boxes with love and care.

Fill in the site name box with 'Joe Blackburn Career Coaching'. I know, I know. That's not your business, but for now, let's use this. You can come back here after Chapter 9 and change it to your chosen name once you've learned the ropes.

Add a tagline in the box: Get a pro Career Coach to inspire you.

Again, let's stick with this tagline for now.

Make sure you fill the WordPress URL and site address URL boxes with the domain name you bought from Bluehost. **This is the real, chosen name you bought.** Also make sure the admin's email address is your real mail id.

Ensure that alongside Membership, the checkbox next to 'Anyone can register' is NOT checked. Letting people in to interact with the site (other than reading) has implications for security. And we don't want to risk going there yet.

Choose your time zone. Instead of the UTC offset, select your nearest city (Los Angeles, New York, etc). City names are tucked away inside the same, long dropdown list, so scroll away to reach them. Select your Date and Time formats. Click on the 'Save changes' button at the bottom.

In the left column click on **Settings > Reading**. Click the checkbox at the bottom of the page against 'Search engine visibility'. We will remember to come here once our site is completed and untick this box.

Right now, since we will be building a fictional career coach's website, we don't want Google and other search engines following us religiously and taking notes. Click on the 'Save Changes' button.

In the left column go to **Settings > Permalinks**. Under Common Settings, you will find the 'Plain' option already chosen for you. Choose 'Post name' instead. This is an important step. Remember to click on the 'Save Changes' button at the bottom.

Cleaning up the themes page

The way your WordPress site appears to the world (once you've built it) depends on the content you put into it as also the theme you use for styling it.

If you click on **Appearance** in the black column on the left, you will be taken to the themes page. The left-most one in the top row is the current, active theme. At any given moment, only one theme can be active and that one controls the overall look and feel of your site.

You will find two or more theme options on the page, depending on what Bluehost decided to install here, which are all currently inactive and serving no real purpose.

Let's clean up this themes page like we did the plugins page. We cleared the plugins page of every plugin in sight. The difference here is that on the themes page, **we clear all themes except for the active theme** (which is a theme called Twenty Twenty-Three.) We will then install our very own theme called **Astra** acquired from the internet for free, and make that active and keep Twenty Twenty-Three as a standby.

Ready? Hover your mouse over a nearby theme that is not the Twenty Twenty-Three theme. Click on the Theme Details box that appears. At the bottom right of the page that appears, look for a tiny 'Delete' link in red. Click on it. Click OK in the confirmation box. It's gone!

Do the same thing with the other extra themes barring the Twenty Twenty-Three theme. Clean up done.

A word about WordPress themes and plugins

What are they, these plugins and themes, exactly? Why do you need them?

Plugins are bits of software that either expand or add functionality to the basic WordPress software. They 'plug in' to the mother software and make it better.

For instance, WordPress is already capable of handling the image needs of your site. However, there are dozens of plugins (mostly written by third-party folks, not connected with the company that makes WordPress) that can give you some amazing and additional image editing and handling capabilities.

Again, if you want to make your website multilingual and make it appear in the visitor's language as they log in from different parts of the world, WordPress by itself cannot do the chameleon dance in real-time. Thankfully, if that's your requirement, there are specialist plugins that can get the job done for you.

How do you go about installing plugins? It's child's play. We will be doing it quite a bit in this book and you will see how simple the process is.

There are thousands of WordPress plugins out there – a big reason for the immense popularity of WordPress itself – and many of them are free. For others, you have to pay an annual subscription. (We will be using only free ones in this book.)

Themes are also bits of software but with a different purpose – to 'decorate' the site with styling. There are hundreds of them out there – some are paid, and many are free.

One main difference between themes and plugins is that you generally have multiple plugins active on your site to help out with various functionalities, but you can have only one theme active at any given moment.

Themes too have to be installed on your website in much the same way that plugins are installed.

We will go ahead and install a free and popular theme called **Astra**, as well as a plugin called **Elementor** (which is crazily a plugin that does the theming! But more on that shortly.)

There is a useful plugin called **Starter Templates** that does a wonderful job of installing both the Astra theme and Elementor plugin at one go while offering us a host of templates to design our pages.

(There is a paid version of this plugin Starter Templates with a gazillion more templates and features but for our purposes, the free one will do.)

And now to install our first plugin that will in turn install the plugin and theme we need.

Installing the Starter Templates plugin

Normally speaking, plugins are plugins and themes are themes. The former for functionality, the latter for styling. But there are a handful of plugins like Elementor that do the styling job of a theme. These go by the name of 'page-builder plugins.'

Since every WordPress site needs a theme that is unambiguously a theme, Astra will do the job for that. Once we install Elementor, it will play well with Astra and generally take over the actual theming of the site in a major way.

If you're asked later what you used to build your site with, you will say, 'Elementor' even though you have Astra installed. It's the way it is.

Back to our narrow black column on the left. Look for 'Plugins' and hover. Click on 'Installed plugins' in the sub-menu that appears. The blank page that shows up is blank because you cleaned it thoroughly a while ago. Click on the 'Add New' button on top of the page to the right of the title 'Plugins'.

You are now on a repository page (on the massive WordPress site) of plugins. Thousands of free plugins live here and we head to the search box on the top right and type in 'starter templates' and wait for a few moments.

The first one that heads the listing is the one we want. It has a good star rating by a few thousand people, 1+ million active installations, and was last updated recently.

This stuff - **star rating, number of people doing the rating, number of installs, and the last update date** - will come in handy to judge the usefulness and safety of all later plugins we install. The better the numbers, the better you will feel about installing them.

Now click on the 'Install Now' button. Once Starter Templates is installed, the button will change to read 'Activate.' Click on it. You'll be taken to your plugins page where the Starter Templates plugin is the first (and only) plugin in the list. Click on the 'See Library' link under the name of the plugin.

The Library has many templates of websites to choose from. Choose a set that is nearest to your needs and you'll have your site ready in an instant!

Well, not so fast. You will have to tweak the content (text and images) to suit your situation, but this is a head start.

Unlike Wix or Squarespace, there is no end to the tinkering and fine-tuning you can do to every aspect of the content and presentation in these templates.

Let's choose a template for our imaginary career coach.

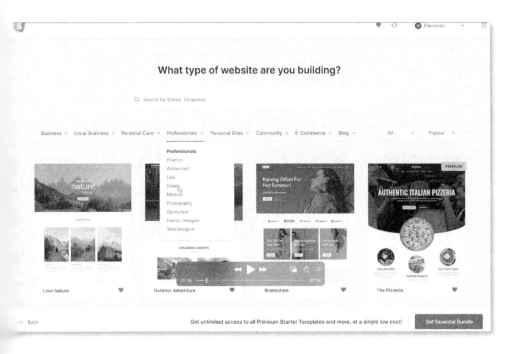

You can make it easy for yourself by clicking on the 'Professionals' link in the top menu and then clicking on 'Coach' from the dropdown menu.

(Because of the endless tweaking you can do, you'll come to realize that you can practically take any template and make it do your bidding. **So don't get too choosy or go necessarily by the name of a template.** We'll proceed with the 'Coach' template in any case, since this is our first time here.)

See the screenshot above.

I scrolled down the page a little and chose the layout that simply read 'Coach.' It asks you to upload a site logo if you wish. We can do this later. Click on the 'Skip and Continue' button to the next page which asks you to change the default colors used by the theme as also the default font pair for the site (one for headlines and one for text.)

I chose the greenish shades as the site colors and also chose the Merriweather–Inter font combination. For now, you can do the same to

see how it all pans out. You can always come back later to change things around. (See the screenshot below.)

Make your color choices and see the page alongside changing its colors in real-time.

Click on the 'Continue' button. Fill in your name, email, and a couple of other details. ' normally uncheck the box that says 'Share Non-Sensitive Data'. Click on the 'Submit & Build My Website' button.

The Starter Templates plugin now goes abou installing the two things we need for our site the Astra theme and the Elemento plugin. When it's done, click on the 'View You Website' button.

Note: If you need click-by-click video guidance in real time for all we've done till now, make sure you **watch the SilentMoves video called SilentMoves Video #1: Elementor - Starter templates install at designWPsite.com/silentmoves.** There's no distracting voice-over, only mouse clicks to clearly show you how to set up and install the Starter Templates plugin.

There it is - **an entire website filled out with dummy content.** You can scroll down the front page to see all the different sections one below the other. You can click on any menu item on top to go to other pages on the site. Just spend a couple of minutes going through the pages and seeing the uniformity in design and color.

We have a full website for a coach using all typical features a coach might need - including a multi-section home page, an about page for his expertise and qualifications, and a contact page with relevant details. All are styled in the site colors and site fonts we chose earlier.

No template however good will exactly fit a real coach's particular needs. We will now go about learning how to modify the content (text and images) on every page to suit our imaginary coach's exact needs.

I advise you to stay in step with me in the following chapters. Do the steps I do, and make the sections and pages exactly the way I recommend. It will help you stay grounded. *It makes sense that your site and my site march forward in an identical fashion and we both end up on chapter 9 with the same result.*

Note: For copyright reasons, I will be using images which I have bought to replace the free ones from the template. You will download images that are royalty-free from sites such as pexels.com, unsplash.com and pixabay.com (explained shortly) to replace the template images with the ones you want.

As you look at the reference visuals in every chapter or the accompanying SilentMoves videos or both, you will be able to readily compare your work with mine and make adjustments as needed. Let's start with our About page next. (Due to copyright reasons noted above, my images will not match yours, but barring that, our sites should be identical.)

Chapter Summary

- You got your SSL certificate from bluehost.com
- You cleaned up the Plugins page
- You set up your details on the Basic Settings pages
- You deleted all themes except the active one on the Themes page
- You learned about the differences between a theme and a plugin
- You installed your first plugin: Starter Templates
- You watched the **SilentMoves Video #1: Elementor - Starter templates install**

◆ ◆ ◆

4. Customizing the About page

PREPARATION: To use the sample content for use with the About page, download the 01-about-page.pdf file from here: designWPsite.com/downloads

Before we edit the About page, it's good to know if we're logged in to our site or not. How do we know that? Look at the space at the very top of your site, whichever page you happen to be on. If you see a slim, black band with some words on it - especially the words 'Howdy, username' on the extreme right - you are already logged in.

If you're saying, "What black band are you talking about?", then it means you're logged out. To log in, type this in the address bar - yoursitename.com/login. Replace 'yoursitename.com' with your site name and follow it up with /login. Hit Enter. From the login page, enter your WordPress credentials and get in.

Incidentally, to log out of your site, click on the 'Howdy, username' link at the extreme right of the thin, black admin bar on top of the screen. From the dropdown menu, click on 'Logout.'

It always happens that when you log in, you get taken to the back end of the site. Click on the extreme left of the admin band on top (yes, that same slim, black band) which has the name of your site. You'll be taken to the front end. Good.

Note: To look at the **finished version of our about page** on your site, visit: designWPsite.com/about-for-joe/. This is the filled-in content and look we are aiming for. (Your masthead image and other images on the page will be different.)

Click on the 'About' link in the main menu of your site. The About page that shows up has already been designed for us. In this chapter, we are going to edit the About page and its sections in ways that might make more sense to our mythical career coach.

To edit the About page, you have to be on the About page on the front end first. Once there, click on the 'Edit with Elementor' link in the black admin band on top of the page (yes, the same one.)

We now find ourselves in the back end of the About page with the content covering most of the page and an Elementor column on the left for making our edits. Whatever changes we carry out in the Elementor column will be instantly executed in the page content.

Between the two columns, midway vertically, there is a small rectangle with a left-facing arrow. Click on it to remove the Elementor column momentarily so that you see the content occupying the entire screen area. Click on that arrow again to get back to editing the page. It's a neat mechanism to check your handiwork as you make progress.

The Elementor column right now displays its 'elements' or 'widgets' - like heading, image, text editor, icon, button, etc. As and when required we will drag any of them onto the main page.

Turn your attention to the content part occupying most of the page. It already has its share of widgets in place - headings, images, body text, etc. Let's try and edit what's there to suit our whim.

For instance, when you **hover your mouse anywhere within the header section** of the content on top of the page (the one with the headline, gradient background, and main image) a blue border encases the section with a 'crown' on top with three icons - a plus, a cluster of dots and an 'x.'

Click on the middle icon - the cluster of dots - **to select the header section.** Watch the Elementor column change instantly.

The Elementor column changes to help you edit the section. The words on the top red band now read 'Edit Section.' Below are various editing controls. See the screenshot below.

This is the main way of working with Elementor. First, you click on something within the content part of the page - a section, a headline, a text box, etc. - and then edit that something inside the Elementor column.

You'll get the hang of this as we work our way through the page.

Editing the header section

We are already in the Edit mode of the header section. We can **change the background image** of the guy in this section with an image of our choice. I used a stock image that I paid for. You can choose one from a free image site (choose a medium size one if you can) or use one of your own.

Click within the header section on the middle icon of 9 dots that's here on top of the section when you hover over it. This selects the section in the Elementor column. Click on the middle button in the Elementor column that reads 'Style.' In the Background section at the very top, click on the image that's already there in the Image box.

You'll be taken to the WordPress Media Library. Drag your chosen image from your desktop (or wherever) and drop it inside the Media Library window. Once the image is added, select it by clicking on it. Click on the 'Insert Media' button at bottom right.

The new image should show up in the content area now. Let's **change the headline text**. We want the new headline to read, 'Prepare well' instead of 'My Story.'

Plus we wish to **insert a button below the headline** as a call to action.

Let's proceed step by step.

To **change the headline text**, click somewhere within the headline in the main section. The Elementor column changes its mode to 'Edit Heading.' You can see it says so in the top red band.

A Title box also shows up below the red band. Type 'Prepare well' in the box after clearing it empty. **Click on the green UPDATE button at the bottom of the Elementor column. Note its position.** You'll keep returning here time and again to save your work. Important!

Adding a button

So far, we edited what was already there – the headline. How do we add something that's not already there?

Like **adding a button** under the headline, for example.

To add a CTA (call to action) button, we need the Elementor column to be in its 'elements' mode rather than the 'edit' mode that it is in currently. Click on the cluster of nine dots in the top red band to the right of where it says 'Elementor'. This is not the earlier cluster of 9 dots on top of section; this is a similar looking one in the Elementor column. It displays the elements or widgets.

Since a button is not among the visible widgets, type 'button' in the search box above. The button widget will come into view. Drag it over to the main content just under the headline 'Prepare Well' till a blue horizontal line shows up. Let go. You'll see a button appear under the headline with the default text of 'Click Here.'

Click somewhere within the button area. In the Edit Button column of Elementor that now shows up on the left, fill in 'FREE CONSULTATION' in the text box against the word Text.

Fill in the **link box** with '/contact' without the quotes so that when someone clicks the button, it will take them to the Contact page.

To change the color of the button, **click on the 'Style' tab** on top of the Elementor column. Click on the globe icon alongside Color under Background Type and choose the Secondary color - a dark grey. *If you want a curved border for your button*, fill in '20' in one of the Border Radius boxes below. (Since the boxes are linked by default, changing the value in one changes the values in all 4 boxes. The 4 boxes are for the four corner values of the button - top, right, bottom and left.)

That will make the button lose its hard edges and become curvy. (In my **SilentMoves video for doing the About page** - link coming up shortly - I kept the button straight-edged, but it's your choice.)

We normally expect a button to change its appearance somewhat when we hover over it. It's called the **hover state** of the button which is a visual confirmation to the user that the button is 'ready' to be clicked.

To get this functionality going, look for the tab that reads 'HOVER' alongside the currently active tab 'NORMAL' and click on it. Click on the globe icon alongside Color under Background Type and choose the Accent color - a middle green. Note that the border-radius values are already filled in, so you don't have to do anything.

Click on the green UPDATE button at the bottom to save your work thus far. To get out of editing the page and viewing it as a visitor would view it, **click on the so-called hamburger icon** (three lines one below the other) in the top red band to the left.

From the menu that appears, click on 'View Page.' It will take you to the front end of the About page.

The top section of the About page is done! It has a revised headline, a new background image and a brand new button that wasn't there to begin with. You have taken small but decisive steps.

There's more to be done. More sections await your editing. To continue your work, click on the 'Edit with Elementor' link on the black admin bar on the front end.

Editing the Main Section

The main section of the template is a bunch of text matter with a headline followed by a short paragraph. This in turn is followed by more text in two columns.

Download the **01-about-page.pdf** file from my website to get your dummy text ready: designWPsite.com/downloads

Need some video help to follow along with this whole chapter? Go watch the **SilentMoves video #02 - Build the About page** over at designWPsite.com/silentmoves.

Let's plan to do a couple of things with the main section.

One: We'll **replace the main heading and the short paragraph** below it with our custom text to better reflect the career coach's details.

Two: Of the two columns of text that appear below, we'll **replace the text in the left column** with our own. Currently, the left column has 5 paragraphs of text. We'll reduce it to just 3 paragraphs.

Three: We'll delete the text column on the right and **replace it with an image** of our famed career coach at work.

Four: Let's add a button with the text 'My Services' that will take the visitor to the Services page for more information on what the coach has to offer. We'll place this button in the left column below the text matter.

Taken as a whole, the Main Section we're planning will start with a custom headline and an accompanying custom, full-width text. Below will be two columns with the left column carrying some more descriptive text and the right column carrying an image. The left column of text will also have a CTA button below it. Got it?

Let's get to work.

To **replace the main heading**, click on the headline 'My Story'. In the Elementor Title box in the left column, replace the words with: 'A job interview is a musical performance.' Click on the green UPDATE button below.

Click somewhere inside the paragraph below the headline. In the left column, you will see Elementor's Text Editor with the current copy in it. Copy the paragraph text from the chapter download and **replace the existing paragraph text** with the downloaded one. Click on the green UPDATE button below.

Now for the two columns of text below. Let's work on the left column first.

If you hover your mouse over the left column up and down, it's easy to see that the left column isn't one block of text. It's 3 blocks of text with a paragraph each. (You can tell by the blue outline boxes that form around the text as you hover.)

Click inside the topmost text block. As before, you'll see the Elementor Text Edit box in the left column. Select all the text and delete it. Paste the custom text you downloaded for this chapter. Click on the green UPDATE button below.

Watch the main content section of the page update itself with the new custom text. Notice that the newly pasted text already has 3 paragraphs, so we don't need the two other text boxes below.

Hover over the paragraph below and a blue border comes into view fencing the paragraph of text. Right-click on the pencil icon in the top right corner of the blue bounding box. Choose 'Delete' from the dropdown menu. Poof, the paragraph is gone.

Similarly, delete the next paragraph below. The left column is now a single block of text with 3 paragraphs of custom copy.

Let's get to work on the right column now.

We have to get rid of the text boxes here before we replace them with an image. Delete the text boxes in the right column in the same way, right-clicking the pencil icon and choosing 'Delete' from the dropdown menu.

To display an image in the right column, we have to get an image from somewhere. A royalty-free site for images is your best bet.

Warning: Don't use any image you find on Google. Most images on the internet are copyrighted, and not meant for free use. You can only use what are called **public domain images** where the author of the image has given you explicit permission for use. It's difficult to know which images are in the public domain and which are not.

Thankfully many websites offer royalty-free images for your use. Some of the well known sites are pixabay.com, unsplash.com, and pexels.com among others.

For our purpose, I used a paid image of a guy in a formal conversation in an office from a stock site. You can download a similar image from a free image site or use one of your own. Make sure it is tall rather than horizontal to fit our layout.

To insert an image, we need Elementor to be in its 'elements' mode rather than its 'editing' mode. If it is in editing mode, click on the cluster of 9 dots on the top red bar to the right of the word 'Elementor'.

You will see the elements or widgets, one of which is Image. Drag the Image widget onto the empty space of the right column and once you see a blue horizontal line that marks the spot, let go.

You will see a placeholder image. In the Elementor column, click in the image box, and from the Media Library import the image of your choice. You can do this by clicking the 'Upload files' tab on the top left and using it to upload an image from your computer into the Media Library.

Click the 'Insert Media' button at the bottom right to display it on the page.

Now for the final touch: a CTA button (call to action) below the text matter in the left column. Follow the same procedure as explained above in the 'Adding a button' section. Hey, this is your practice exercise, go for it. The only difference here is that the text on the button should read 'MY SERVICES' and the link should be '/services' (without the quotes.)

Of course, there's always the SilentMoves video to guide you, just in case.

Note: If you need click-by-click video guidance in real time, make sure you watch the **SilentMoves video #02 - Build the About page** over at designWPsite.com/silentmoves. There's no distracting voice-over, only mouse clicks to clearly show you how to edit the About page from top to bottom.

Editing the Feedback Section

The next section that is titled by the template as 'Feedback & Reviews' is a useful one for our career coach to display a couple of client testimonials.

I'm not going to change the text matter here as you may have guessed from the absence of a text download for this part of the About page. We already know how to change headlines and replace text matter. No point in doing more of the same thing. (Feel free to change it to text of your choice, though.)

So let's pretend that this Feedback & Reviews is all fine with our career coach just the way it is as far as the content goes.

Instead, let us use this section **to learn about text alignment** – how things like text boxes and headings can be aligned to match the overall layout of a page. This is a handy skill to learn, as you will have to constantly align stuff in different parts of a website to make it all look consistent.

You will notice that the title 'Feedback & Reviews' is center-aligned on the page. Which is not the alignment we've enforced thus far. We have been left-aligned throughout. So let's align the title and the little copy matter beneath it to align to the left of the page.

Click anywhere inside the title. In the Title box in the Elementor column, notice the 'Alignment' parameter at the bottom. Click on the left alignment icon, the first from the left.

Now click anywhere in the tiny paragraph underneath the title. The Text Editor in the Elementor column this time offers no alignment help. You'll have to click on the 'Style' tab on top. You'll find Alignment right on top of everything else. Click the left align icon. (Why the alignment icons are sometimes at the bottom and sometimes at the top, I have no clue. The words rearrange to the left, but the entire paragraph is nowhere close to the left edge of the page in the way that the title is. What's going on here?

The paragraph as a whole has a huge left margin which has to be eliminated.

How? Stuff like **margins and padding** determine the spacing around an element. These values are found in the 'Advanced' tab on top of the

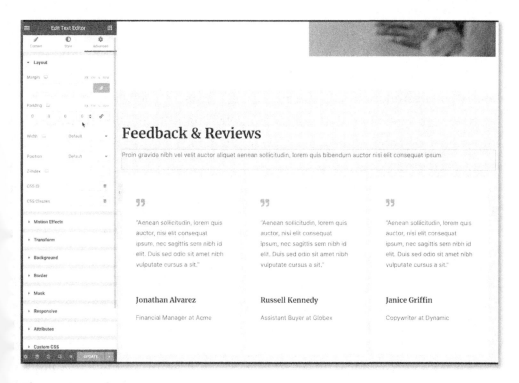

Elementor column.

Click on the 'Advanced' tab. You'll notice that the Padding field already has numbers allotted. The four boxes, from left to right, are for the padding spaces at the top, right, bottom, and left. See screenshot above (with zeroes filled in.)

There is a link-like icon on the far right of the padding row which can be turned off or on by clicking on it.

'On' means all 4 values are linked and can be changed in one go by altering a value in any box. 'Off' means the values are not linked. Typing a value in a box will only change that value and not change other values in other boxes.

For our purpose, just clicking the link icon on puts zeroes in all the boxes. And the paragraph loses its padding and aligns itself perfectly to the left in line with the title.

Onward, then.

We have 3 identical boxes of text to deal with next. Each box has a quotation mark symbol on top, the actual testimonial text, a client's name, and their designation. All of these 4 elements in each box are center-aligned. Let's get them left-aligned one by one. I'll take you through the procedure for the first box. You can apply it to the other two boxes in an identical manner.

Click next to the quotation mark. In the Icon box that appears in the Elementor column, you'll find the Alignment settings at the bottom. Click on the left-align icon. The quote on the page moves to the left.

Click somewhere inside the testimonial text. Look to the Text Editor in the Elementor column. There is no Alignment setting here. Click on the 'Style' tab on top. Set the Alignment setting to left by clicking the left-align button. Click inside the client name. In the Title box on the left, click on the left-align icon.

Click inside the designation text. In the Text Editor in the left column, you will find no alignment settings. Click on the 'Style' tab on top. Set the alignment to left by clicking the left-align button.

Your turn now. Do the remaining two boxes of text and get all elements within them left-aligned. If you're as paranoid as me about losing hard work, click the green UPDATE button to save your work thus far.

The above instructions may appear tedious to read and follow. Watch the **SilentMoves video #02 - Build the About page** over at designWPsite.com/silentmoves to see how simple this really is.

There is a section titled 'What Can I Do for You?' below. We decide that our career coach has no use for this section because whatever he wanted to say on this page is already said. So hover your mouse within this section, wait for the blue border to appear, and click on the 'x' on top to get rid of it.

Click on the UPDATE button one final time for this page. Go to the far left at the very top of the Elementor column and click on the 3-lined hamburger icon there. In the menu that appears, click on 'View Page.'

You'll be back on the front end of the About page. Scroll down and up to admire your handiwork. The About page is now done. Joe Blackburn thanks you for the tremendous work you've put in.

Chapter Summary

- You learned how to log in and log out of your site
- You put in custom text for the headline
- You added a button or two
- You edited paragraph text
- You added an image to the main section
- You learned about using royalty-free images
- You left-aligned icons, paragraphs, and headings
- You watched the **SilentMoves video #02 - Build the About page** over at designWPsite.com/silentmoves

◆ ◆ ◆

5. Customizing the Services page

PREPARATION: Use the sample content with the Services page. Download the 02-services.zip file from here: designWPsite.com/downloads

B efore we proceed with designing the content and styling of our Services page, we have to go on a detour.

We have to activate certain settings that affect the whole site globally and not just this page or that.

Remember that the following few paragraphs on **global settings** do not apply exclusively to the Services page. They apply to the entire site.

Global settings: Placing our logo

Global settings are those settings that affect the entire site at one go.

Changing global settings like logo placement in the header or editing the green bottom section (the one just above the footer at the bottom of every page) is done using the Astra theme rather than Elementor. At least the free version of Elementor does not do headers and footers.

Barring a couple of instances of global settings (not all, just the couple we will be discussing shortly) we will not be dealing with other Astra settings in this book.

Let's **change the logo** - something that affects the entire site, whichever page you happen to be on. From the front end (any page), on the thin, black band at the very top of the site (called the admin bar) click on the site name on the far left.

That will get you to the admin section, or back end, of the site.

In the narrow black column on the left, look for 'Appearance' and hover your mouse over it. Click on the 'Customize' link in the sub-menu that appears. (The SilentMoves help video for this section takes off from this point onwards.)

As you can tell by the look of the menu on the left, this is not the Elementor Edit page that we used before. This is the Customize Page of the site theme Astra.

Click on 'Header Builder' in the left menu. Now click on 'Site Title & Logo.' Click on the 'Change Logo' button. It will take you to the Media Library.

Here you can upload the fictitious Joe Blackburn's logo using the 'Upload files' tab on the top left. (You will find the .jpg logo when you unzip the file you downloaded for this chapter. Ignore the fact that I'm uploading a different logo in the help video. This is the **SilentMoves Video #03 Global settings** at designWPsite.com/silentmoves.)

Download the **02-services.zip** file from here: designwpsite.com/downloads

Click on the 'Select' button at the bottom right to insert the logo onto the page.

Switch off the slider button next to 'Different Logo for Retina Devices?' Click on the 'Publish' button on top.

Note: For click-by-click video guidance in real time, watch the **SilentMoves Video #3 Global Settings** at <u>designWPsite.com/silentmoves</u>. It will show you all the moves discussed above to set up the site logo and also edit the bottom section (discussed below).

Global settings: Editing the bottom section

Click on the left arrow to the left of 'Header Builder' on top to go back one step. Click on **'Footer Builder.'** To edit the bottom section, hover your mouse over the green background in the main content portion of the screen till you see a small pencil icon on top of the text matter.

Click on the pencil.

You may have to sometimes click once more on the pencil icon to see the screen as shown below. The left column shows a Text box with a Title box and an empty text box below it.

Copy the Title text from the chapter download file and paste it into the Title box (after deleting the current Title there, of course.)

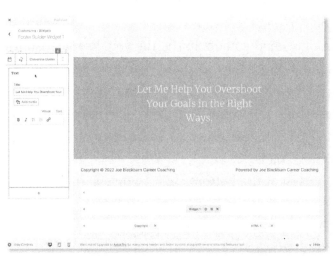

The new Title should read: *18 years in Fortune 50 companies as recruiter | 12 years as Career Coach | ICF Certified | Author of the best-selling book 'Yes You Can Kill The Interview.'*

Leave the text box below empty. Click on

the 'Publish' button on top of the left column.

Take note that **there are 3 horizontal white bands** in the main part of the page at the bottom. You can see them below the green section we just edited. Taken together, the 3 bands represent a maximum of 3 sections you can stack one on top of another to form the Footer.

The top band is empty. The next band says 'Widget 1' which happens to be the green section we edited moments ago. The bottom band has two columns 'Copyright' on the left and 'HTML 1' on the right. They represent the bottom-most section of our site carrying the copyright message.

Let's understand what's going on here and see what we can influence. Click on the 'Copyright' button (but not on the 'x' alongside, you will delete it!).

The left column displays an edit box. The text in the text box reads Copyright © [current_year] [site_title] - there's your first glimpse of some WordPress code!

Not to worry. It should be simple enough to make sense of. The words inside the square brackets are dynamic code - **they enable WordPress to pull in the value of the current year as also the site title and display them without you having to type them out**.

With each passing year, the copyright year displayed will change automatically. Neat, right?

Similarly, if you click on the 'HTML 1' button you will see the text box reading: Powered by [site_title]. We can leave this also alone for now.

(Later, when you get to designing sites for others, you can change this message to something like 'Designed by Linda Thomas' - if your name happens to be Linda Thomas, that is.)

Since we are done here, click on the 'X' on the top left in the left column. It will take you back to the Dashboard. Click on the site name in the black admin bar above the 'Dashboard' label. See the newly minted logo showing up nice and bright on the front end.

Now that the site logo and the bottom footer section are in place, let's get back on track with the main task: Building the Services page.

Getting 'Services' item on the Main Menu

Before we surge ahead with full-on confidence and positivity to fashion our new Services page, **let's take a step back**. We notice that the main menu on the site has a menu item called Courses. Clicking on it is what got us here to the Courses page.

We can start by getting 'Courses' off the menu and putting in its place a new menu item called 'Joe's Services.' Makes sense? Let's do it.

Since we are already on the Courses page, **click on the 'Edit page' link** in the black admin bar on top. Read that again.

Note that we're NOT clicking on the 'Edit with Elementor' link as before, but the 'Edit page' link. Why is that?

Because we want to get to the original WordPress page rather than Elementor's Edit page. We want to make a couple of basic content changes on the WordPress page itself.

One, we wish to change the title of the page which is currently 'Courses'; and two, we wish to change the permalink or the URL of the page. (You can't do either of those things using Elementor, not easily at any rate.)

Click in the Title box on top and delete what's there. Type 'Joe's Services' in the box. Next, look at the column on the right. Click on 'Permalink.' The URL slug box currently reads 'courses'. Delete that and type in 'services.'

Click on the blue UPDATE button on the top right of the page. In the **black band that appears at the bottom of the page**, click on the 'View Page' link. It will take you back to the front end of the page.

Note: This black band stays on screen only for a few seconds. If it disappears before you can click it, just click the Back button on the browser to get you to the original page - and refresh it. All should look normal, except...

...the menu item no longer reads 'Courses'. It is now 'Joe's Services.' A great start!

To follow the steps above to get 'Services' onto the main menu, you can watch the **SilentMoves Video #4 Services in Main Menu** at designWPsite.com/silentmoves for click-by-click help.

Planning our Services page

Let's say our career coach has three coaching services to offer his clients: Mid-Level Interview Coaching, Senior Level Career Coaching, and Executive Coaching. He wants to talk about each service along with a key visual.

After pondering on what to feature on the Services page, we decide on the following sections:

· A **masthead or hero section** with an image and headline, similar to the one on our About page

· A **services section** that highlights the 3 service offerings we noted above

· A **testimonials section** that showcases quotes from our satisfied clients

· A **book section** that features the career coach as a prominent author in the field with a purchase link to Amazon

We can use the template site's Courses page (which we just renamed) as a starting point. Click on the 'Joe's Services' link on the main menu.

You can tell that this page doesn't quite have all the things we want. We have to tweak it to our liking. And that's the main purpose of this chapter. To make a random template page bend to our will.

The masthead or hero section on the Courses page already has a full-width background image and a headline on top of it. We know how to change the image as well as rewrite the headline. So that looks doable. Great.

Just below, there are as many as six content blocks, each with its image and write-up. In our mind's eye, we can adapt these blocks to display our service offerings rather than courses. We can also reduce the number of blocks to three from six. Fine.

But the Courses page doesn't offer any help for the other sections we need - a testimonials section and a book section. There's nothing here for us to tweak. **Instead, we have to add two new sections that aren't there.**

It's in situations like these that we get to appreciate the strength and flexibility of the Elementor + Starter Templates combination. We can not only edit or delete sections (as we already saw earlier), but we can also add brand new sections on any page (as we'll see shortly.)

Note: To look at the **finished version of our services page** on your site, visit: designWPsite.com/services-for-joe/. This is the filled-in content and look we are aiming for. (Your masthead image and other images on the page will be different.)

Hero section: Changing the background image

Let's return to the back end of Joe's Services page. Click on the 'Edit with Elementor' link this time in the admin bar above.

Before we change the background image, let's make a familiar and easy alteration. Let's change the words of the headline. Click on the headline. In the Title box in the Elementor column, type in (or paste) the new headline: Joe's Services.

Onto the background image. Let's change the background image here to something else you might already have or get from a free image site like pexels.com or pixabay.com.

In the main part of the page (not the Elementor column), hover your mouse in the masthead (hero) section and click on the Edit Section icon (the middle icon with 9 dots at the top of the blue bounding box.)

In the Elementor column, click on the 'Style' tab on top. Click on the Image box below. It will take you to the Media Library. Click on the 'Upload files' tab on the top left and select an appropriate file from your computer to upload. I used a paid image of a woman in an interview situation from a stock image site. You can use your own or get one from a free image site like pexels.com or pixabay.com.

Note: While I will be covering details of **how to optimize images** for the web in Chapter 9, for now, download images that are not too big. For masthead purposes, something like 1280px x 800px or thereabouts should do. The pexels.com site calls this size 'Medium' and that should be fine. For other uses where the image doesn't need to go full-width, a 'Small' will do just fine.

Once uploaded, select the image and click on the blue 'Insert Media' button at the bottom right to place it on your page. Click on the green UPDATE button in the Elementor column at the bottom. You can click on the little eye-icon to the left of the UPDATE button to preview the page with the changes done so far. This will open the site in a new tab.

Or, click on the hamburger icon (three lines one below the other) in the top red band to the left. From the menu that appears, click on 'View Page.' It will take you to the front end of the Joe's Services page - but in the same tab that you're on now.

Editing the 3 Services section

For a help video on the previous masthead (hero) section and this services section, watch the **SilentMoves Video #05 Masthead & services** at designWPsite.com/silentmoves.

The next section below the hero section is headlined 'My Courses.'

Click within or next to the headline. In the Title box that appears in the left column, type in (or paste) the new headline: Career Services At Every Stage. Click on the left-align button in the Alignment row at the bottom.

Similarly, click within the paragraph beneath the headline. In the Text Editor on the left, delete the existing text and replace it with the downloaded text for this chapter.

To left-align this text, click on the 'Style' tab on top and click on th left-align button there. Even that may not do the full job of pushing th text matter entirely to the left (as we saw before.)

Click on the 'Advanced' tab on top and reduce the left padding to zero The text should align correctly now. Click on the green UPDATE button a the bottom. **We will use the top row of 3 Image Boxes (as Elementor call them) to talk about our three service offerings.** We will delete the bottor row of 3 more Image Boxes shortly for we have no use for it.

An **Image Box** is a composite of different elements. Each Image Box has an image, a title, and a description. Of course we could have always dragged in the individual elements or widgets ourselves to create an 'Image box' - an image widget, a headline widget and a text editor widget and stacked them. It's just that, as a convenient feature, Elementor combines them for us and gives it to us as a ready-made Image box.

We will edit one Image Box together and you can similarly do the other two Boxes. That will be your exercise. (Wink, wink. There's always the SilentMoves video you can view for help.)

Click in the first image box. The Edit Image Box settings open in the left column. Click on the tiny image there to change it to an image that you downloaded from a free-image site. (Use a 'small' size.)

Next, click in the Title box and type in (or paste) the new headline: Mid-Level Interview Coaching. In the description below, you can copy-paste the text from the downloaded text for this chapter. You will note that all these changes in text and image are being reflected in the main content on the right side of the page in real-time.

Your turn now. Edit the remaining 2 Image Boxes.

Hover your mouse over the next row of 3 Image Boxes such that a blue border appears encapsulating all of them. Click on the 'x' on top of the blue border to get rid of this row once and for all. Click on the green UPDATE button as usual to save all your changes. Go to the front end and view Joe's Services page. So far so good.

Note: For click-by-click video guidance on the above sections completed so far, watch the **SilentMoves Video #05 Masthead and services** at <u>designWPsite.com/silentmoves</u>. It shows all mouse clicks discussed above.

Now we need to add a couple of **new sections**: one for client **testimonials** and another for the **book display** that dear Joe has written. There's no section from the template that matches our requirements.

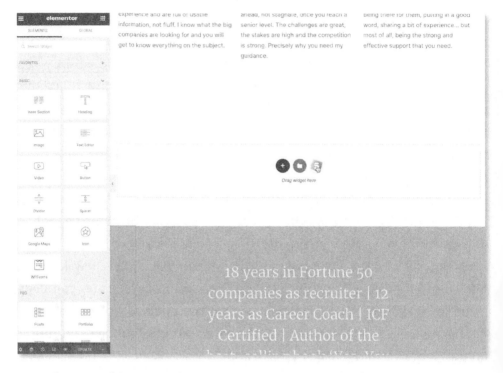

In fact, on this page, there is no section left at all for us to manipulate its settings. We have to create a brand new section or two instead of editing what we already have. How do we do that?

Creating a new section: Testimonials

The Starter Templates plugin we installed comes to our rescue. If we get to the back end of the Services page and scroll down, we see a blank space below the main services section we just edited. The blank space carries three icons in the center of the page: a plus icon, a folder icon, and the Starter Templates icon. See the screenshot above.

Click the Starter Templates icon on the right. You'll be taken to a template library, featuring many pages and blocks. It's the blocks that we are after. Click on the 'Blocks' tab on top.

In the dropdown menu at the top left of the screen, choose Team among the various categories listed. I chose the second option on the page for our section by clicking on it.

You now get a close-up view of the chosen block. If you're satisfied with it, click the blue button on the top right that reads 'Import Block.' This inserts the block onto the page.

We can change the heading that reads 'Secondary Heading.' Change it to: 'What my clients say...' We do this the usual way by clicking on the headline somewhere and using the Text Editor box on the left to make the text changes.

Similarly, we'll change the descriptive text beneath the title to what we want it to be. Use the downloaded text for the chapter here. You can use the alignment tricks we learned earlier to left-align both the headline and the description.

Hint: Because the layout for this block uses a column within a column called an Inner Section by Elementor, you will find that our earlier alignment tricks get us only so far. That's OK for now.

Change the images with your own as before. Keep the text beneath the images (provided by the block template) or put in some text of your own (if you need the practise.) We know by now how to change both images and text.

Click on UPDATE as ever to save your work. Watch the **SilentMoves Video #06 Testimonials and book at** designWPsite.com/silentmoves to create the testimonial section as well as the book section coming up.

Creating a new section: Book display

We have one more section to go: a write-up on Joe's book and the cover image. We would ideally like a section (or a block, as Starter Templates calls it) to have two columns - one for the cover image and another alongside for the text including headline and copy.

We can do the same thing we did with the previous testimonials section. We can get into the Starter Templates library and look for an appropriate block. But in this case, it is unlikely there is a block template for our specific use case of showcasing a book cover with some copy next to it.

It's faster to **make our own custom section or block**. It's also a useful skill to learn for the times when you don't get a ready-made block for something special you want to accomplish. In the white space below the testimonials we just finished, you'll find the same 3 icons as before: a plus icon, a folder icon, and the Starter Templates icon.

Click on the '+' icon this time to add a new section. What comes up is a set of structure options to choose from. How many columns do you want? In what proportion? Choose the one that has a thin column on the left and a fat one on the right.

You will get two blank columns with a '+' in the center of each - they are waiting for you to add something into the blank areas. Mouse over to the Elementor column and click on the dot cluster on the top red band to the right of the word 'Elementor.' That brings to view all the elements you can choose from to fill up your blanks.

Grab the Image widget and drop it inside the thin, blank column. Click on 'Choose Image' in the Elementor column. From the Media Library insert the book cover image you downloaded from the assets for this chapter. This should be a familiar drill by now.

Grab the Heading widget and drop it into the fat, blank area. Click inside the headline and change the text to the text you downloaded for this chapter: 'The Last Word In Interview Coaching.'

Grab the Text Editor widget and drop it below the heading in the fat, blank area. Click inside the text and replace the dummy text with the downloaded text for this chapter. If you watch the SilentMoves video for this section, you'll see I've used some stylistic devices to make the various parts of the text stand out as bold, italic, heading, etc. Use them if you want the nuances.

Drag a **button element** from the Elementor column and drop it below the text next to the book image.

Click on the button icon. Make the text read 'Buy on Amazon'. Leave the link box with a '#' – it's a placeholder that doesn't go anywhere, a dead link till you replace it with a real one once you know your Amazon book page.

Note: For click-by-click video guidance, watch the **SilentMoves Video #06 Testimonials and book at** designWPsite.com/silentmoves. It shows all mouse clicks discussed above.

Remember to click the green UPDATE button to save your work. Click on the eye icon next to it to preview the page. If you find (as I did) that the spaces between this section and the two sections above and below it are too narrow, here's how you can **increase the space between sections**.

Get to the back end with the 'Edit with Elementor' link on the admin bar. Hover in the book section area till a blue border appears around the section. Click on the 9-dotted icon on top of the border to edit the section.

In the Elementor column, click on the 'Advanced' tab on top. Adjust the padding top and padding bottom to 100px after turning off the link button on the extreme right.

(If the link button is on, as you will remember, all the values will change to 100px. You don't want that.)

The final section for the Services page is done.

If you pause and mentally take a few steps back, you'll notice new lessons here. You learned how to change a background image (top section), how to use block templates (testimonials section), and how to create a custom section from scratch (book section).

It's what you might call a productive day.

Chapter Summary

- You learned about global settings and changed the logo
- You edited the bottom section as part of the footer settings
- You edited the hero section - revised the headline, changed the background image
- You edited the Image Boxes section to turn 'courses' into 'services'
- You created a new section for testimonials using a Starter Template block
- You created a custom section with 2 columns for book content
- You watched 4 SilentMoves videos: **Video #03:** Global settings, **Video #4:** Services in Main Menu, **VIdeo #05:** Masthead and services and **Video #06:** Testimonials and book

◆ ◆ ◆

6. Finalizing the Contact page

PREPARATION: There is no sample content to download for the Contact page.

T oday is when we do the Contact page in quick time and also clean up the main menu on the top of every page.

Note: To look at the **finished version of our contact page** on your site, visit: designWPsite.com/contact-for-joe/. This is the filled-in content and look we are aiming for. (Your masthead image will be different.)

Let's start with the menu clean-up.

Editing the Main Menu

As already noted, Elementor doesn't do the header and footer. And the Main Menu is inside the header section.

So we have to edit the Main Menu in WordPress or the Astra theme instead of using Elementor's Edit screen.

Hover your mouse on the black admin bar on top, at the extreme left where the site name is. From the dropdown menu that appears, click on 'Menus.' It will take you to the Menus page of WordPress. Note that there is no Elementor column on the left.

You will see the menu items listed one underneath the other in the main, bigger part of the screen. Click on the down arrow next to e-Books. We don't need this page because we have no use for it. Click on the red 'Remove' link and - poof! - it's gone.

Next, by way of ordering the menu, grab the 'Joe's Services' menu item and drag it up underneath 'Home' and above 'About.'

Click on the down arrow next to 'About' and in the Navigation Label box replace 'About' with 'About Joe.' We're trying to be on a friendly, first-name basis here.

Now that we're done, click on the blue 'Save Menu' button on the lower right of the page. You'll be taken to the front end. And you can confirm the newer, crisper, well-ordered Main Menu in plain sight.

Note: For click-by-click video guidance, watch the **SilentMoves video #07 Edit the Main Menu** at designWPsite.com/silentmoves. It shows you all the mouse clicks discussed here.

Editing the Contact page

Already, the Contact page provided by our template looks all set to go. All the ingredients are there - a welcoming intro, a mail id and phone number, a contact form, and some helpful text on the side. What's to complain?

Perhaps we can change the person's image at the top but beyond that there's nothing much to do with the content matter.

We know how to change the top image. We look for the top section's blue border and click on the 9-dotted icon at the center of the three icons at the top of the border.

The Edit Section opens up in the Elementor column. We click on the middle tab on top - the 'Style' tab. We click on the tiny background image there and from the Media Library, we upload a visual we like. I used a paid image from a stock site. You can use something similar or different as you like.

For the intro text under the 'Get in touch' heading, use some sample text of your own. Or use something like what I used in the video lesson. Not that it makes a huge difference, but it gives you more hands-on practice in editing text.

As my SilentMoves video shows, I also changed the phone number and mail id a little to remind you how it's done. Click the green UPDATE button to save your work.

Note: For click-by-click video guidance, watch the **SilentMoves Video #08 Edit the contact page** at designWPsite.com/silentmoves. It shows all the mouse clicks.

All is good so far. Do you want to talk about the elephant in the room? It's the contact form! It's sitting pretty in plain sight, yet the **contact form can only be edited outside of Elementor**.

By 'edited' I mean adding a new field like 'Phone' or deleting an existing one like 'Subject.' Such things can be done only within a plugin called **WP Forms** and not directly on the page.

You see, when we installed our first plugin Starter Templates, it installed (as already noted) the Elementor plugin as well as the Astra theme for us. What it also did was quietly install another plugin called WP Forms (free version). This is a popular plugin to generate forms (like our contact form) for use on our site.

If you think about it, such forms not only have to display fields like name, email, etc. but **they also have to do something**. When a visitor fills up the form and clicks on the Submit button, their details and message have to be mailed to you as the site owner.

The default mail that a visitor's message gets sent to is the **admin email of the site** which is something you decided when you set up WordPress with Bluehost.

If you're wondering where that admin email resides on your website, go to the backend of your site and click on **Settings > General** from the left, black column. You'll see your admin email there. That's the mail id to which our contact form will sent its messages.

That's the process. Let's edit the contact form now.

Editing the Contact Form

Let's say you want to **delete the 'Subject' field**. Not many sites have this field these days and it's one less field for the visitor to fill up. That's more inviting for a prospect to send the form.

Where do you go to make this deletion? Get out of Elementor by clicking on the hamburger icon (3 lines) on the left of the red band on top and then clicking 'Exit to Dashboard.'

From the left column, hover over the WP Forms menu item and click on 'All Forms' from the fly-out menu that appears.

On the page that now appears, crowded with copy, it's easy to miss the 'Contact us' form near the center of the page. See the screenshot below.

When you hover over it, a tiny menu appears underneath. Click on 'Edit' in the tiny menu. You will see the form fields big and upfront displayed on the next page. **Hover over the Subject field and click on the**

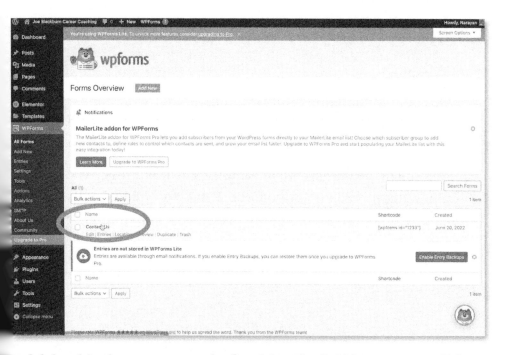

red delete bin that appears on the far right. The field is gone. Now click on the orange 'Save' button on the top right of the page.

The job is done. But for your information, it may be useful to know that if you click on the 'Settings' item in the far left vertical menu you will see 'Notifications' as a menu item in the new menu alongside. Click on 'Notifications.' Under Default Notification, you can change the Send To Email Address from {admin_email} to some other email of your choice. Remember to click the orange 'Save' button on top when you're done.

Note: For click-by-click video guidance, watch the **SilentMoves Video 09 Edit the Contact Form** at <u>designWPsite.com/silentmoves</u>. It shows all mouse clicks discussed above.

Get back to the front end and review your handiwork. The Contact page is done. **Fill in the form and send a message to yourself** to check it works properly.

Chapter Summary

- You edited the main menu items in the WordPress back end
- You changed the background image in the masthead
- You edited the text matter in the intro section
- You learned about WP Forms
- You edited the WP Forms contact form and deleted the 'Subject' field
- You watched 3 SilentMoves videos: **Video #007**: Edit the main menu, **Video #08:** Edit the contact page and **Video #09**: Edit the Contact Form

◆ ◆ ◆

7. Creating the Home page

PREPARATION: To use the sample content for use with the Home page, download the 03-home-page.pdf file from here: <u>designWPsite.com/downloads</u>

I think it's a great idea to build the Home page last. Once you know what goes into the other pages and what they look like, it becomes easier to build the Home page.

Think of the **home page as a content sampler to the various pages** within the site while also serving up the main benefits of doing business with you.

Note: To look at the **finished version of our home page** on your site, visit: designWPsite.com/home-for-joe/. This is the filled-in content and look we are aiming for. (Your masthead image and other images on the page will be different.)

Editing the Hero section

From the home page on the front end, click on the 'Edit with Elementor' link in the admin bar above. Hover the mouse over the hero section and once the blue border around the section appears, click on the middle icon (with the 9 dots) at the top of the border.

In the Elementor column on the left, click on the 'Style' tab on top and then the tiny image. From the Media Library choose the image you want for this section and click the 'Insert Media' button. I used an interview situation of two people shaking hands from a stock site (paid image). You can get a free one from pexels.com for now. (Again, download the 'Medium' size image.)

It is useful to know an interesting tweak you can do to this image or images in general. **Under the various settings under the image in the Elementor column, you will find 'Size' which is by default set to 'Cover.'**

Almost all of the time, this setting of Cover will serve your needs best, but occasionally a setting like 'Contain' or 'Auto' may be perfect for a particular situation depending on the image you upload and its dimensions. Experiment.

To change the headline and the description text below it, you already know the drill. Click into them, one after the other, and make the changes in the Elementor column. Use the copy matter that you downloaded for this chapter.

Download the **03-home-page.pdf** file from here: designwpsite.com/downloads

Click on the left button that reads 'Start Now.' In the Elementor column change the Text to 'Get in touch' and link it to the Contact page And for the other button, change the text to read 'Know more' and link it to the About page.

Note: For click-by-click video guidance, watch the **SilentMoves Video #10 Home page hero section** at <u>designWPsite.com/silentmoves</u>. It shows all mouse clicks discussed above to complete the hero section.

Editing the Process section

In the template version of our home page, there is a slim section underneath the main hero section with logos which serves no purpose for us. We can remove it by hovering over the section, and clicking the 'x' icon once the blue border appears.

Similarly, we can delete the 'What I do' portion and the 3 green boxes of text below it. However, we want to keep the two-column structure below the green boxes though (the one where the left column headline reads, 'Need advice?' and the right column headline reads, 'My e-Books & Courses.' We want these columns.)

The catch here is that these 3 mini-sections - the 'What I do' part with the tiny paragraph below, the 3 green boxes of text, and the 'Need advice?' bit - are all part of the same section. So if you delete the section you'll lose the 'Need advice?' bit and the adjoining column as well. You don't want to do that.

So you have to delete the green boxes section first. Then the headline next. And lastly the paragraph of text. Watch the SilentMoves video to be clear about this.

Note: For click-by-click video guidance, watch the **SilentMoves Video #11 Home page process section** at <u>designWPsite.com/silentmoves</u>. It shows you how to complete the process section. To get the dummy content to use, download the **03-home-page.pdf** file from here: <u>designwpsite.com/downloads</u>

Now edit the left column ('Need advice?) in three parts - the headline, the body text, and the button. These changes are no different from any of the copy edits we've made so far in other sections and other pages.

Use the downloaded copy. Link the 'Call me' button to the Contact page.

Similarly tackle the right column too in 3 parts. Use the downloaded copy as text. Link the 'Know more' button to the Services page.

Yet again, watch the SilentMoves video if you're in any doubt on how to go about this.

Click on the green UPDATE button to save your work. Go to the front end to check your handiwork on the page thus far.

Creating the Testimonial section

The next section in the template is a Testimonial section, but **we are going to delete it and bring our testimonial block** in from the library.

Why? Because it's nicer to have a testimonial with the supporting image of the person rather than an impersonal graphic of a laptop.

The other reason is to get more practice for bringing in blocks from the library.

Hover over the current Testimonial section but don't delete it. Instead, click on the '+' icon on the top of the blue border to add a new section.

Click on the right-most Starter Templates icon to get into the library of both page templates as well as block templates.

Since we want blocks, click on the 'Blocks' tab on top. In the dropdown menu to the far left, choose 'Testimonials.' I used the single testimonial block as shown in the screenshot below. (If in doubt, check the block I've used on my home page at designWPsite.com/home-for-joe/.)

Once the block appears on your page, click inside the text matter and change it in the Elementor column with the copy you downloaded for this

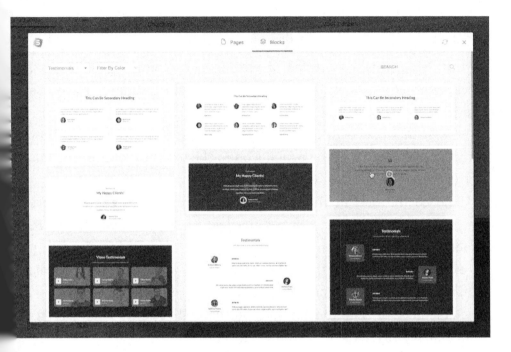

chapter.

Change also the name and the designation to get some editing practice. Change the photo with an image of your choice. Click the UPDATE button.

Scroll down a bit and delete the original Testimonial section by clicking on the 'x' on the blue border of that section. Be sure to save your work by clicking on the green UPDATE button. Click on the three-lined 'hamburger' icon on the top left of the Elementor column and choose 'View Page' to get to the front end. Survey your work this far.

It's coming along nicely, isn't it?

Note: For click-by-click video guidance, watch the **SilentMoves Video 12 Home page testimonial** at <u>designWPsite.com/silentmoves</u>. It shows you how to complete the testimonial section.

Editing the About section

The next section in the template is the About section with a photo and a write-up of the site owner. This works well for us.

The left column, in terms of elements, contains a headline, a text block, another text block and a button. The right column is of course an image.

Using the text editing tricks we've learned, delete the bottom paragraph of text using the pencil icon in the top right of the blue border box. (Right-click and delete.)

Replace the text in the remaining text block with the downloaded material for this chapter. Change the text on the CTA button to 'More About Joe.' Link the button to the About page.

Replace the image in the right column with an image of your choice - either your own photo or an image from a stock site.

Remember to click the UPDATE button and review your work on the front end. We're racing to the finish line now.

Note: Watch the **SilentMoves Video #13 Home page about section a** designWPsite.com/silentmoves. It shows you how to complete the Abou section.

Creating the FAQ section

For most sites, a Frequently Asked Questions section is a great ide Having introduced your key promise, supporting facts, main offering and client testimonials, a small business can put itself in the shoes of i customer and answer key concerns and doubts.

The FAQ format is a familiar and reassuring device that tackles user needs head on. It tells the customer what to expect when they deal with you.

Generally, **a FAQ section on the front page can have between 4 and 8 questions**. If your business requires a more exhaustive list of questions to be addressed, it's better to have a separate and dedicated FAQ page rather than cramming everything onto the front page.

For our site, we'll have a brief FAQ section. Get to the back end of the front page through the 'Edit with Elementor' link as usual. Beneath the About section ('My Story') we just finished, you'll find the theme's 'Drag your widget here' section. Click on the Starter Templates icon on the right.

See the screenshot.

Click on the 'Blocks' tab at top of the page. From the dropdown menu at the left, scroll down to FAQ and click. From the various options, I chose the block with 4 questions at the bottom.

See the screenshot.

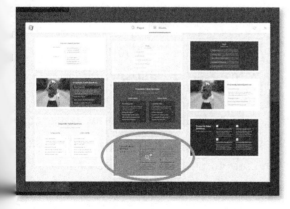

From the close-up page of the chosen block, click on 'Import Block' button on the top right.

Use your text editing skills to change the 4 questions to the text you downloaded for this chapter. (I didn't bother writing out the answers, though - mainly because I didn't know what they were!).

Also, change the text under the title to what's there in your downloaded file. Remember to save your work with the green UPDATE button. **Note:** For click-by-click video guidance, watch the **SilentMoves Video #14 Home page FAQ section** at <u>designWPsite.com/silentmoves</u>. It shows you how to complete the FAQ section.

Go to the front end and scroll down to see this section as a visitor would. And know that not only is this section and this page now finished but...

...**the entire site (minus the optional blog) for our career coach is now finished!** You deserve some serious congratulations for sticking on and getting this done. You also deserve a break.

Chapter Summary

· You edited the Hero section with a new background image, headline, text, and buttons

· You edited the Process section by deleting and revising

· You brought in a new Testimonial section with Starter Templates blocks

· You edited the About section with custom text and button

· You created a new FAQ section with a Starter Templates block

· You finished the basic website for the career coach!

· You watched 5 SilentMoves videos: **Video #10:** Home page hero section, **Video #11:** Home page process section, **Video #12:** Home page testimonial, **Video #13:** Home page about section and **Video #14:** Home page FAQ section

◆ ◆ ◆

8. Creating a Blog (optional)

PREPARATION: To use the sample content for use with the Blog page, download the 04-blog-pages.pdf file from here: <u>designWPsite.com/downloads</u>

Wordpress started life as a blogging platform. If you want to include a blog on your website, it's easy enough as we'll see in this chapter. If you have no use for a blog, skip this chapter.

Strangely, a popular page builder like Elementor - the free version - has no features to offer us. There are no nicely designed pages to drag across or cool-looking blocks to bring over.

You need the paid version of Elementor to get all the extra blogging features including spiffy layouts. If yours is primarily or heavily a blogging site, you'll want to look into the paid Pro version of Elementor.

We will continue to use the free Elementor builder on our site, forgoing the bells and whistles. For most normal sites that also include blogs as against being predominantly blogging sites, this should be nicely adequate.

To get our blog going, **we will use WordPress's page builder called Gutenberg**. Gutenberg comes with WordPress, so there's nothing new to install. It works similar to Elementor in that you can insert pre-made blocks (elements) into the layout.

What we call a blog is basically a collection of individual blog posts written over time, often by the same author. Copy the first blog post from the downloaded text for this chapter. We are going to create our first blog post. Ready?

Creating a blog post

Get to the backend of your site. **Click on Posts > Add New**. Paste the headline from the downloaded text (blog post #1) into the title box. In the blank box below the title, copy-paste the text matter for the blog post. Yup, the whole thing.

It's a good idea to watch the SilentMoves video that goes with this part of the chapter.

Note: For click-by-click video guidance, watch the **SilentMoves Video #015: Create a Blog** at designWPsite.com/silentmoves.

It shows you how to create the Blog section.

Once you place the text matter for the main body of the blog, it's time to format it.

Note: To look at the **finished version of a typical blog post** on your site, visit: designWPsite.com/website-question-1-how-many-pages-should-i-have/. This is the look we are aiming for. (Your featured image on the page will be different.)

As a visual device, we can make use of a couple of divider lines above and below the first line of copy. To do this, click in the space in front of the first letter of the first line. Press Enter or Return to push the text to the next line while creating an empty line on top.

Click on the '+' button that shows up to the right of the box that is now empty. Type 'separator' in the search box to **find the divider block or element**.

Click on the Separator icon (you don't have to drag it over, just clicking on it will do.) A line appears inside the empty box.

Click in the space to the right of the last character of the first line of copy - the full stop - and press Enter or Return. This creates an empty box below the line of text. Using the '+' button in this box, click on the Separator icon again to get a horizontal line inside the empty box.

Select all the words between the two horizontal lines. From the contextual menu that appears, click on 'B' and 'I' to make the text both bold and italicized.

Now for **styling the sub-heading**. Find the line that reads "The 4-5 page structure" and select it. Click on the left-most icon in the contextual menu that appears. It's the 'Transform' icon (see screenshot below.)

From the dropdown menu, click on 'Heading'. It will automatically make the sub-heading in H2 format. Since this is too big, change it to H3.

Click on 'H2' in the contextual menu and you will see other options. I found that the H3 setting was perfect for our needs.

You can similarly format a couple of more sub-headings to H3 down the page. You can also select the very last line of copy that talks about the 'Next part' and click on the 'I' button in the contextual menu to make it italic.

As a blog grows over time with the addition of more and more posts, it is customary to **group posts into categories**. It is also good practice to start a blog with some categories in mind and start associating each post with one of them.

Let's assign a category to this first post we've just created. If you want to take your blog seriously and build it over time, organizing individual blog posts into categories is a must.

In the right column, as you scroll down, you will see 'Categories' (which you may have to click on to open the section if it isn' already open.) Click on 'Add New Category' link and type in 'WordPress' to signify this post is about WordPress tips.

Why a career coach will want to write posts on WordPress is just the kind of inconvenient question we don't want to ask right now.

To add the category, click on the 'Add New Category' button below. This will add the category to your blog (and also place a tick mark beside it to assign it to this post) and this category option will be available to every post you create from now on.

Blog posts also generally have a main image or a lead image that goes with them.

WordPress calls it a **'featured image.'** If you scroll down the right column a bit more, you'll find a grey box with the words 'Set featured image.' Click on it.

You'll be taken to the Media Library which you have visited a few times before. Select an image that you may have already uploaded here. Or, use the 'Upload files' tab to freshly upload an image from your computer to the Media Library. Then click on the 'Set featured image' button at the bottom right to bring it into your blog post.

We now have everything that we want in our post - the main heading or title, the main text (formatted with bold and italics as called for), the sub-headings, a stylistic device like a separator, a chosen category, and a featured image.

It's time to **publish the post**. Click on the blue 'Publish' button on the top right of the page. You'll have to click on it twice. At the bottom you will see a black band with a 'View Page' link. Click on it to go to the front end and see the blog post.

What you see on the front end has the featured image prominently at the top with the title below it. Below the title is the 'meta' information - category, author name, and the date. The full text should follow below it. Note the H3 sub-headings.

Cool? Now it's your turn.

Using the same techniques, **create the remaining 4 blog posts using the downloaded text for this chapter**. Assign them all to the category of 'WordPress' and use your own visuals which you can get from pexels.com or a similar site.

You must create this handful of blog posts. You need **a set of blog posts in place to create a 'Blog' page on your site** which will feature excerpts from your recent posts with thumbnail-sized featured images.

So get to work and copy-paste (as also stylize) the additional blog posts before getting to create the blog page as explained below.

Creating the Blog page

To create a Blog page that contains excerpts from your latest blog posts, WordPress requires us to **create a new blank page** (not a post.)

You can title this blank page anything you like: My Coaching Advice, Latest in the Coaching World, My Expert Comments, and so on. We will title this page simply 'Blog.'

Remember, we are not creating a post. We are creating a page that will hold all our post excerpts. That's the way WordPress rolls. And it's been doing it for decades.

Once ready, this page will display a listing of brief excerpts of your blog posts, appearing in reverse chronological order. Which is a fancy way of saying the more recent posts get shown first.

We then link this blog page to an item called 'Blog' in the main menu. Visitors click on that, get on to the blog page, review the excerpts and click on any of them to explore a specific blog post in its entirety.

Let's **create the Blog page** then. Go to the backend of your site and click on Pages > Add New from the left column. In the title box, type 'Blog'. That's it.

Don't do anything else. Save it by clicking on the blue 'Publish' button on the top right twice. You're done.

What? How does this work? There's nothing on the page! How will it display the blog excerpts? WordPress works in mysterious ways. What you're about to do in the next step below turns this blank page into a page like no other. It truly becomes our Blog page.

Here's the magical next step (see the screenshot below.) Go to the backend and **click on Settings > Reading**.

Against 'Homepage' you can see that the page 'Home' has been chosen. But against the 'Posts page' nothing has been chosen. Click on the

dropdown menu and select 'Blog' which is our designated page for 'holding' blog posts.

Click on the blue 'Save Changes' button at the bottom.

Now click on **Pages > All Pages** in the left column. You will see all the pages your site contains. In the SilentMoves video, you will see that I delete the pages called 'e-books' and 'Sample Page.' You can do the same as demonstrated in the video, for these pages serve no purpose for us.

Note: For click-by-click video guidance, watch the **SilentMoves Video #015: Creating a Blog** at <u>designWPsite.com/silentmoves</u>. It shows you how to create the Blog page.

You will see the page 'Blog' in the All Pages listing. Hover over it and see a sub-menu appear beneath. Click on 'View' to see the main blog page on the front end.

And - voila! - this empty blog page is no longer empty. It is anything but. **All the excerpts are there from each of the 5 blog posts you created.**

Note: You can see the **finished version of the Blog page** at: designWPsite.com/blog. Compare it with your own blog page. Close enough?

A neat little column on the right displays the recent posts as a list of titles. Your visitors can now click on any of these post titles (either in the main section or in the right column) and be taken to the relevant blog article in depth.

Now that the Blog page is ready, let us **link this page to a menu item on the Main Menu** at the top of every page.

Click on the site name on the far left of the black, admin band on top. From the dropdown menu that appears, click on 'Menus.' You'll be taken to the Menus Edit page.

In the left column look for the Blog page. If you can't see it there, click on the next tab that reads 'View All.'

Click on the checkbox next to Blog to tick it. Click on the 'Add to Menu' button below to add it.

Watch it appear in the listing of menu items on the right part of the page. You can grab the Blog rectangle with your mouse and drag it a couple of places above, just below Joe's Services. Click on the 'Save Menu' button at the bottom right.

Get back to the front end. And you should see the main menu now featuring the Blog item as well. Click on it. And you should be on your Blog page. Click on any title. And you should be taken to that blog post.

The blog feature on your website is now in place.

Chapter Summary

· You learned about the Gutenberg page builder that comes with WordPress

· You used Gutenberg to create and stylize your first blog post

· You learned how to assign a category to a blog post

· You uploaded a featured image to go with your blog post

· You created 4 more blog posts and formatted them

· You learned how to create a Blog page and made it display your blog post excerpts

- You added a 'Blog' menu item and linked it to the Blog page
- You watched the comprehensive SilentMoves **Video #015**: Create a Blog

◆◆◆

9. Let's add some nice-to-have features

PREPARATION: To use the sample content for use with this chapter download 06-favicon.png file from here: designWPsite.com/downloads

O nce your website's main pages are complete, you wil inevitably feel the need to make it better. By adding extra littl things like social media icons, comments in blogs, a way fo visitors to fix phone appointments with you, and so on.

We will cover such additions in this chapter to make the site full featured. I suggest you still **stay with the career coach pretense** and finis the site. Once you know the tips and tricks, it's a simple matter to appl them to your own content and layout.

Now that the meat-and-potatoes stuff of what a website should be over, this chapter looks at nice-to-have features to make your websi appear that much more professional in feel and finish. Feel free to ac whichever of these catches your fancy.

Adding social media links

Social media links are of two kinds: **Follow** and **Share**.

Follow links are little icons on your site (in the header or footer usually) that link visitors to your social media pages. If you are active on Twitter and LinkedIn, for instance, you'll have these two icons on your site to let your visitors 'follow' your activity.

Share links are little icons on your site (at the end of an article or blog post usually) that *link visitors to their own social media pages.* If a visitor finds an article or a post interesting, they can share it with their social circle on FaceBook, Twitter, or wherever by clicking on that icon.

Let's **add some Follow links** to our site. A good place to add your Follow links is the footer. Since the footer occurs on all pages of the site, you effectively make your links available throughout your site.

We can use the footer space that currently has the default lettering of 'Powered by Joe Blackburn Career Coaching' over in the right column. **We can replace it with a set of social media icons** of our choice.

If you remember, the header and footer are controlled not by Elementor but by the main theme Astra. From the front end, click on 'Customize' in the top admin bar to get us into the Astra edit area.

From the left column, click on 'Footer Builder.' Click in the empty space to the left of 'HTML 1' in the bottom row of the main part of the page. A menu will pop out from which you select 'Social.'

If you scroll to view the footer in the main preview window above, you will see that a row of social icons has appeared below the 'Powered by...' line. Since we don't want this line anymore, you can go down to the last row of the editing area and click on the 'x' of the 'HTML 1' box to get rid of it.

Check the preview area above and you'll find the space now only holds our social media icons and nothing else. Click on the pencil icon as you hover in that space. The left column will show the 3 default icons of Facebook, Twitter, and Instagram. To delete any of them, click on the 'x' to the right of their names.

Click on a name like Facebook and fill in the URL box below with the address of your Facebook page. (Copy that from the address bar by visiting your FB page.)

There is a dropdown menu with other popular social options like LinkedIn, Behance, etc. Click on any of them if it is relevant to you. Click on the blue 'Add Social Icon' button alongside the dropdown. Fill in the correct URL for the new icon.

Remember to click the blue 'Publish' button on top to save your settings. You can check on the front end by going to any page and seeing that the social icons are in place in the footer.

Note: Watch the **SilentMoves Video #16 Social media icons** at designWPsite.com/silentmoves. It shows you how to create follow links in the footer section of every page.

Setting up the site's favicon

Let's set up our site's favicon now.

A favicon is a tiny graphic that shows up in the tab of a browser. In Chrome, for example, the favicon for YouTube shows up in the tab as in the screenshot below.

A favicon's job is to tell you which site is where at a glance when you have multiple browser tabs open.

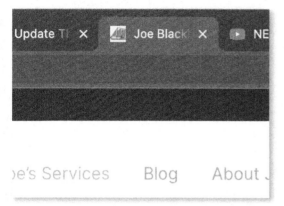

It's the kind of detail that goes toward making our fledgling site look professional. Like the Follow Links feature we discussed earlier, favicon editing comes under the Astra theme rather than Elementor.

For this exercise, you can use the site icon I have given as part of your content download for this chapter. Or you can create a simple graphic that represents your site. It can even be the starting alphabet of your site name in an interesting and bold font style.

You can use a free online program like Canva to create your favicon. Since the final display is going to be small, **keep the design extremely simple.**

Let's get to the Astra edit page. Click on the 'Customize' link on the admin bar on top of any page that you are on.

In the left column, click on 'Header Builder' and then on the 'Site Title & Logo' link. At the bottom of the Logo edit screen click on 'Site Icon' link. Then click on 'Select site icon' box.

In the Media Library select the favicon you created and uploaded. Click on the blue 'Select' button at the bottom right. Click on the 'Publish' button on top of the left column and you're done.

(I have included a tiny favicon for your use at designWPsite.com/downloads. Feel free to use it if you don't want to create one yourself.)

Exit the Astra edit page and look at the tab of your site. It should carry the icon you just inserted.

Note: For click-by-click video guidance, watch the **SilentMoves Video #17 Favicon for your site** at <u>designWPsite.com/silentmoves</u>. It shows you how to create a favicon for your site.

Inserting a video

We have no video displays of any kind on our site. What if you want to show a video on a page to illustrate a point you're making? This could be a video by a celebrity in your field or created by you.

If you want to display your own video(s) on your site, make note of the following point.

Unlike images, which you upload to the Media Library, **you don't upload video files to your own website**. Video files are huge and take up a lot of space. Your cheap hosting plan will probably not have enough resources to store and stream videos without a glitch, especially when many visitors land simultaneously.

Besides, with sites like YouTube and Vimeo doing the dedicated business of hosting videos, you are better off uploading your videos there. **So if you're going the route of making your own videos, host them (for free) on YouTube.**

All you then need to figure out is how to link such videos uploaded on YouTube to your website. Linked properly, a preview of your video will show up on your site. When a visitor clicks on the play button, the video plays right there on your site, although in reality, it is YouTube that is streaming it.

If you're using someone else's videos to illustrate your points, it's the same procedure. Get the video link from YouTube and paste it into your page to make it show up there (we'll see in a moment how to do that.)

Note: Unlike images, you don't have to worry about copyright or permission to display a YouTube video on your site. People upload public videos on YouTube presumably to get more and more exposure. By linking,

Danza Castellana by Torroba | DuJu

our site is doing them a favor by giving them more exposure.

So how do we get a YouTube video to play on your site? Let's say you want to link to a specific video on YouTube from one of your blog posts. The method is the same whether it's a blog post or any other page of your site.)

The first step is to go to the desired video page on YouTube. Copy the address of the page from the address bar on top. It will be in the form of "https://www.youtube.com/watch?v=stringofcharacters." This is the video link we need. See the screenshot above.

Back to your site. From the main blog page, reached by clicking 'Blog' on the main menu, click on any blog headline from the posts featured there. You'll be taken to that blog post in its entirety.

Click on the 'Edit post' link at top of the page. Click at the end of any paragraph and press Enter to create a new empty line where you want to insert the video.

Click on the '+' button within the blue border and type in 'video' in the search box. The YouTube block will show up. Select it and in the URL box paste the video link you saved.

Click on the blue 'Embed' button to the right.

The video preview will spurt to life right there.

Click on the blue 'Update' button on the top right of the page to save this new setting.

Go to the front end of the blog post to check. Your video is now ready and in place, for all the world to see.

Note: For click-by-click video guidance, watch the **SilentMoves Video #18: Insert a video** at <u>designWPsite.com/silentmoves</u>. It shows you how to display a video on your blog post.

Setting up comments for your blog

If you choose to have a blog on your site, you can invite comments or keep it all closed. Some prefer to give out their tips, advice and observations without allowing for feedback of any kind. Others prefer two-way communication with their visitors.

My suggestion will be to **have comments on your site if you're having a blog**. Interaction helps, gets user engagement, and is good for search engine optimization. If you're worried about spam or undesirable comments, there are solutions to avoid both, discussed below.

Setting up comments on a WordPress site is an on-off thing that is currently switched off by default. To turn comments on, do the following.

If you're on the front end of your site, click on the site name in the black admin band on top to the extreme left. Once in the dashboard, **click on Settings > Discussion** in the left column.

Against the Default post settings, tick the checkbox for 'Allow people to submit comments on new posts.' And against the 'Before a comment appears' section tick the checkbox for 'Comment must be manually approved.'

This ensures that comments are not automatically published once someone submits them (you don't want to publish spam posts.) Instead, every comment is submitted for moderation by you.

You get a notifying email that someone has put in a comment. You can first review it and then publish it (or not.)

Click on the blue 'Save Changes' button at the bottom of the page. Get to the front end. When you get to any blog post now, you will notice there is no change at all!

It's because the **setting that you switched on adds the comments feature to only new posts**, not to already existing ones.

It's not a problem, though. Go to each post and click on the 'Edit post' link in the admin bar. It takes you to the WordPress backend (remember, blog posts don't come under Elementor) for that post.

Scroll down to the right column and in the Discussion section, **tick the box for 'Allow comments.'** Update the page and the post will now have a form section below to take in user comments.

To stop spam (or more accurately, reduce spam considerably), you can install a plugin. The best one is an anti-spam plugin called **Akismet**. It is free for non-commercial use but if you're in any kind of business, you'll have to pay ($99 per year.)

The other plugin (free) I've found quite useful is a plugin called **Stop Spammers** which is just something you install, and activate and that's just about it. No settings to tweak or anything. Plug and play.

The installation is straightforward, like any of the plugins we've installed thus far.

Click on **Plugins > Add New** from the left column in the back end.

Type in Stop Spammers in the search box, wait for the plugin to appear, click on 'Install' followed by 'Activate', and you're done. See the SilentMoves video if you need help with this. The plugin installation comes toward the end of the video.

Note: For click-by-click video guidance, watch the **SilentMoves Video #19: Set up blog comments** at <u>designWPsite.com/silentmoves</u>. It shows you how to activate the comments feature for your blog and also install Stop Spammers plugin.

Adding a button to the Services page

It always happens that when you review a page that's finished, you wish you could add a couple of more things to it.

On our Services page, for instance, we can add a button for the hero section on top - a CTA button to urge action ('Make an Appointment').

Makes sense, right? Let's do it.

Go to the Services page on the front end. Click on 'Edit with Elementor' link on the top admin bar. Once at the back end, make sure the Elementor column on the left is showing the Elements tab with little rectangles like Heading, Text Editor, Image, Video, etc. If you're not seeing this, click on the little icon of a collection of 9 dots on the top right of the Elementor column.

Click in the hero section anywhere. Then use the Elementor search box on top to type 'button'. Once the button widget shows up, drag and drop it under the headline within the hero section.

Click on the button icon and in the left column fill in the Text with 'MAKE AN APPOINTMENT'. You can insert your Calendly link (see next chapter) in the Link text box. (You can leave it with the default '#' for now. Come back later and fill in the Calendly link when you have one.)

Use the other controls, if needed, to set anything else you want. Once done, click on the green UPDATE button at the bottom.

Note: If you don't know what Calendly is, see the section 'Taking appointments on the website' in the upcoming Chapter 10. You can return here to connect the popular app with your website, once you learn about it.

Click on the green UPDATE button to save your work. Go to the front end to check all is hunky dory.

See the SilentMoves video for any help or clarification.

Note: For click-by-click video guidance, watch the **SilentMoves Video #20 Adding button to a page** at <u>designWPsite.com/silentmoves</u>. It shows you how to add a button to the Services page.

Showing the Bottom section only on some pages

If you took a glance at all the pages of the site so far, you will notice that the green Bottom section (with the enlarged copy highlighting key selling points) is present on every page of the site. This is overkill.

For instance, on the Contact page, there is this big Bottom section that feels unnecessary. Certainly, on the main blog page as well as on individual blog posts, this section has an intrusive, misplaced quality to it.

So, long story short, **how do we show this Bottom section only on some pages** we want to and not on other pages we don't want to?

You may remember that this section was created and controlled as part of a generalized page footer. Since a footer by default shows up on all pages of a website, the Bottom section too shows up everywhere.

You may also remember that the Bottom section was out of the scope of Elementor and we handled it with our Astra theme.

Unfortunately, in this case, **Astra does not allow us to display this section selectively** on some pages and not on others. The workaround is that we delete the Bottom section from Astra so that it shows nowhere at all!

We can then create our own Bottom section using Elementor only on those pages we want it to display. Clear as mud? Read on, it will all fall into place.

From the front-end, click on 'Customize' on the admin bar to get into the Astra edit page. Click on 'Footer Builder' link in the left column.

In the main part of the page, you will see a page preview under which you will see three white bands. The middle band holds our Bottom section with something called 'Widget 1'. Click on the 'x' next to it to delete the section. (Before you do that, make sure, you've saved the text matter that goes into the Bottom section.)

Click on the 'Publish' button on top of the left column. Close the section and review it from the front end. The Bottom section has vanished from all pages of the site!

Let's now recreate the Bottom section on only the Services page. Go to the Services page and click on 'Edit with Elementor' link on the top admin bar. Scroll down to the area below the book section.

In the space where you see the 3 icons, click on the Starter Templates icon on the right. Choose the Blocks tab on the next screen and from the dropdown menu on the left, select 'About'. From the various options, I

chose the simple, single-column layout. See the screenshot.

Get this block into your page by clicking on the Import Block button that appears after you select the block.

You can see that this block has 3 mini-sections of text within it: a subheading, a big heading, and some tiny copy matter. Let's delete the subheading by clicking on it and right-clicking the pencil icon in the blue bounding box that appears. Select the 'Delete' link at the bottom.

Similarly, get rid of the tiny text matter. **All we have left is the main heading.**

Replace the words with the selling-points text we had before (you saved it somewhere, didn't you?) Now click on the 9-dots icon in the center of the section on top of the blue bounding box.

In the Elementor column, click on the Style tab. Against Color, click on the globe icon and select the color for the background for the section.

See the SilentMoves video for the mouse clicks and moves.

Note: For click-by-click video guidance, watch the **SilentMoves Video 21 Show/hide section** at <u>designWPsite.com/silentmoves</u>. It shows you how to create the Bottom section on the Services page.

Click on the green UPDATE button as always to save your work. Check your work on the front end and ensure the new Bottom section shows up in the Services page.

Create a similar Bottom section on the About page as an exercise for you to complete. It should be a cakewalk for you by now. (**Hint:** You can **watch the same SilentMoves video** above to learn how to do this on the About page in a similar manner.)

Cheers. You're done with all the add-ons for your site.

Chapter Summary

- You set up social media follow links in the footer
- You created and displayed a favicon for your site
- You learned how to insert a YouTube video into your page or post
- You activated the comments feature for your blog and installed an anti-spam plugin
- You added a button to the Services page
- You restricted the display of the Bottom section to only the Service page (plus the optional About page)
- You watched 6 SilentMoves videos: **Video #16:** Social media icons **Video #17:** Favicon for your site, **Video #18:** Insert a video, **Video #19:** Set up blog comments, **Video #20** Add button to a page and **Video #21** Show hide section

◆ ◆ ◆

10. Important finishing touches

In this final chapter of learning WordPress with Elementor/Astra, we will talk about important finishing touches and techniques. These are essential to most websites and you should include them in your own website once you learn how.

- Optimizing images (what it is and why you should do it)
- Creating a Privacy Policy page (what it is and why you should have one)
- Enabling appointments on your site and integrating with the Calendly app (optional)
- Installing 3 important plugins for your site's safety, speed, and backup (important!)
- Testing your site's speed (why and how)

Let's start with optimizing images. What exactly does this mean and why optimize images at all?

Optimizing images on your site

The bigger the image, the greater its resolution and the better it looks. But it comes at a cost - every hi-res image file is close to 1 MB if not more. That is simply too huge a size for website usage.

Every image bank out there like pexels.com, unsplash.com, shutterstock.com, etc. - there are hundreds of them - will give you hi-res images each of which can be anywhere between 1 MB and 25 MB. Even your phone camera produces pretty large images.

By website standards, these are huge files to store in a database and serve to every visitor who comes calling at your site.

If the images on your website are ridiculously high in file-size running into many MBs, that page will take forever to load. On the other hand, smaller file-size images make for a smooth and fast website.

Optimizing an image means reducing its size. And size can mean one of two things:

Dimensions: An image that is 600 x 400 px (width x height measured in pixels) is preferable to an image that is 4800 x 3200 px.

Density or file-size: An image that is 250 Kb is preferable to an image that is 3 MB (file size measured in Kb or Mb.)

Before you upload an image to the Media Library it is good to get into the habit of noting its dimensions and file-size.

To make an image usable for your site, you have to therefore **reduce its dimensions** to some optimal size, depending on how big you need it on the page. Plus, you also have to **reduce its file-size** by using a process that is known as **'compressing.'**

Once you've done both, you have optimized an image for web use. It's a crucial part of site building. It's easy to learn this skill with a few online resources to help you.

Let's say you have a horizontal image that you downloaded from a site like pexels.com or something you shot yourself. Its dimensions are 4000 px by 2500 px and its file-size is, let's say, 1.5 MB.

As always, you have a SilentMoves video to guide you through the process once you get the hang of it here.

Note: For click-by-click video guidance, watch the **SilentMoves Video #022: Optimize images** at <u>designWPsite.com/silentmoves</u>. It shows you how to optimize images for use on your website.

You know by now that all these numbers are way above optimal. Consider the width of a normal computer. It is something around 1300 px perhaps. If an image's width is 4000 px that is certainly overkill even if you wanted it to occupy the full width of the screen.

And the density of 1.5 MB is way over the limit for a single image. Let's get to work.

Go over to **iloveimg.com** which is one of many such sites that can get the job done for us. I like its simplicity of use. Click on 'Resize Image' link in the main menu or in the display below the menu.

Grab the humongous image from your computer and drop it here. Or click on the blue button that reads 'Select Images' and upload.

You'll see some resize options in the right column. The image file's original dimensions are filled in already. Reduce the width from 4000 px to 1140 px. Note that the height also proportionately reduces (keep the box 'Maintain aspect ratio' below checked.)

Click the blue 'Resize Images' button below.

The resized image should **auto-download** now. The reduction in dimensions is now done. One part of our job is complete. Now, onto compressing the image next.

For this, I prefer a site called **tinyjpg.com**. Its service is free up to a maximum of 20 images per day (at the time of writing.) It's totally easy to use.

Just drag our image (with the reduced dimensions) into the box on top of the home page at tinyjpg.com. The compression is done in a few seconds. Click on the download link alongside and you're done.

Your image is now reduced in dimensions and also compressed. The optimization is done.

In the instructional SilentMoves video, you'll find that by doing the above, an image that was 4000 px by 2500 px and a file-size of 1.3 MB got optimized to 1140 x 700 px and a file-size of just 99 KB.

Read that again. It's 99 KB, not MB. Such an image can be put up for full-width use, like in the hero section of any of our pages. For other parts of a page, you can go for smaller dimensions like 800 x 600 px or 600 x 400 px, etc. And your site will load fast!

While there are plugins to get automatic re-sizing and compression done, their effects are sometimes unreliable. I find that a few moments of dragging and dropping images in small batches on these two sites give great results.

And you don't have to think of them again, once they are optimized and uploaded to your site's Media Library.

As a thumb rule for what file-size works best, **consider 250 Kb as the number to remember**. Don't let any image go over that and it often should be much below that.

You will also develop a sensibility over a few weeks on what sizes work well on different parts of a page. This is invaluable expertise.

Creating a Privacy Policy page

Of all the so-called legal pages many websites tend to have, the very minimum is the Privacy Policy page.

Even if you don't do e-commerce or anything complex on your site, a Privacy Policy page is necessary, and legally required in many countries. If your site has a basic contact form and/or comments turned on for its blog (both true in our case), you are collecting user data, whether you think of it that way or not.

Someone is giving your their name and email at the very least and possibly a comment or two for your blog.

The issue is what you are, or your site is, planning to do with this user data. Why are you asking for it? What do you intend to do with it? What if a user asks you to remove all their data from your site? How would you respond to that?

And so forth. Your Privacy Policy page sets out, in concrete, the answers to concerns like these and more.

Since I'm not a lawyer, I'm not qualified to give you advice on what exactly you should or should not include on your Privacy Policy page. Google to your rescue! (Ask your lawyer to vet it if you want to be extra careful.)

I have found the site **https://termly.io** useful and easy to use. You answer a series of questions that pertain to your website and by the end of it, it gives you the text which you can copy-paste onto your website.

Where exactly do you paste this on your website? **On a new page that you create specifically for this purpose.** Let's do it.

Go to the back end and click on Pages > Add New. Enter the title text as 'Privacy Policy' and paste the copy you have chosen in the text area. Click the 'Publish' button. You're done.

The link to this page is generally placed in the footer so that it is 'reachable' from every page of your site. From the front end, click on 'Customize' to get to the Astra back end.

(Remember, the header and footer details are not managed with Elementor but with Astra.)

Click on 'Footer Builder' link and then on the 'Copyright' box in the last row of the main part of the page. Type in 'Privacy Policy' after the copyright message in the text box and give it a link using the 'Link' button.

(Select the words Privacy Policy and click on what looks like a paper clip icon. Put in the address of the link, something like '/privacy-policy' will do (without quotes.)

Click on the 'Publish' button on top and you're done.

Taking appointments on the website

Generally speaking, most sites have a contact form on their Contact page. A visitor gets there either from the main menu and/or gets directed from other pages through a call-to-action button.

Typically these buttons read 'Contact Us' or 'Contact Me.' And this setup is fine.

These days, an option that is becoming popular is to have the button read 'Make an appointment' or 'Call me'.

This link does not go to the Contact page on our site, but a third-party appointment site like calendly.com. Once there, on your Calendly page your visitor can choose from an online calendar and fix their appointments for a certain day and time.

Calendly allows you as the site owner to set up date and time slots that are convenient to you. The visitor has to merely choose one of those defined slots. Appointment fixed!

Watch the SilentMoves video on how to register for a free account on Calendly and set up your time slots. It's a fairly simple process and you are perhaps already registered with this popular app.

You will also get **a special link to your appointments page on Calendly**. Copy that and use that to link your CTA button on any page of your site with the app. (See the 'Adding a button to the Services page' section in Chapter 8 for details on how to do this.)

Note: For click-by-click video guidance, watch the **SilentMoves Video #23: Fix appointments** at <u>designWPsite.com/silentmoves</u>. It shows you how to get the link to the Calendly app. You can then re-visit your Services page backend and fill in the link to the button on the masthead that reads, "Make an appointment."

3 basic hygiene plugins for your site

One of the last things you should do on your website after everything is done is to safeguard it. You want **to provide a firewall** around it making it tough for bots to break in. You want to ensure your **site loads fast** and doesn't dawdle for long with clicks.

And you want to **take periodic backups** of your site and store them somewhere handy. In the event of - God forbid! - a site crash, you can always restore the original site from the latest backup.

For reasons of safety, speed and backing up, I consider the 3 plugins below as basic hygiene. Your site shouldn't go out and present itself to the world without these in place.

There are other options to these plugins - and good ones at that - but I think these 3 are truly top of the class. Free versions of these plugins are sufficient for our use.

Wordfence for security

The installation of this plugin is like any other. In the WordPress backend, click on **Plugins > Add New** and when taken to the WordPress plugin library, type in 'wordfence' in the search box.

When it appears, click on 'Install' and then 'Activate.' Usual stuff, right?

When you're taken to the back end of your site, Wordfence will ask for your email and try to sell you its premium (paid) version.

Click past them (see the SilentMoves video if you need help) and you'll land on the Plugins page.

In the left column, you will find a new entrant 'Wordfence' in the menu.

Click on **Wordfence > Dashboard**. From the plugin's dashboard, in the Firewall section in the top half of the page, click on 'Manage Firewall' link.

On the next screen, click on the button that reads 'Click Here To Configure.' Click on 'Continue' button in the popup box and you're done setting up the plugin.

Note: For click-by-click video guidance, watch the **SilentMoves Video #24: Wordfence for security** at <u>designWPsite.com/silentmoves</u>. It shows you how to install the Wordfence plugin for use on your website.

WP-Optimize for caching (speed)

Similarly, install and activate the free plugin WP-Optimize from the plugin library. Once you're back on the WordPress plugins page, you will see the new plugin listed among all the others you have. Click on 'Settings' under the plugin name.

From the menu on the top right, click on 'Database' to optimize the database for your site. Click on the blue button that reads 'Run all selected optimizations.' Wait for a few moments till it's done.

Click on 'Cache' from the top menu. Switch on 'Enable page caching'. Click on 'Save changes' button at the bottom. You're all set with this plugin.

Note: For click-by-click video guidance, watch the **SilentMoves Video #25: WP-Optimize for speed** at designWPsite.com/silentmoves. It shows you how to install the WP-Optimize plugin for use on your website.

Updraft Plus for backing up your site

Install and activate Updraft Plus from the plugins library as usual.

Once you see the plugin in your plugins list, click on 'Settings' under the plugin name. You will land in the Backup/Restore tab of the plugin's dashboard. Click on the 'Settings' tab. From the first drop-down menu for files backup, choose 'Weekly' and retain 3 backups. Use a similar setting for the second dropdown menu for database backup.

Below, you will see a list of **possible storage options** you can use for backing up your website. The free version of Updraft Plus, the one we're using, allows only one of these storage options to be chosen.

Google Drive is the popular one and almost everyone has their drive with their stuff on it. Click on 'Google Drive' and then go all the way down to click on the 'Save Changes' button. You will be asked to sign in to your Google account if you aren't signed in already.

Follow the instructions and your Google drive will be 'connected' with your Updraft Plus plugin. Every week, your site will be backed up automatically to your Google drive.

The last 3 saved backups will be preserved, so you don't take up inordinate space on your drive. You can breathe easy now. Your site is safely stored.

Watch the SilentMoves video for help if you need it.

Note: For click-by-click video guidance, watch the **SilentMoves Video #26: UpdraftPlus for backups** at designWPsite.com/silentmoves. It shows you how to install the Updraft Plus plugin for use on your website.

Testing your site speed

Once you are happy with your site build, you should test its speed. A popular and reliable measure of site speed is **GTMetrix**. Go to gtmetrix.com and put your site URL in the box and hit 'Test your site' button.

You will get to see the key metrics. If everything is green, you are in a good place.

Note: For click-by-click video guidance, watch the **SilentMoves Video #27: Testing with GTMetrix** at <u>designWPsite.com/silentmoves</u>. It shows you how to test your website loading speed.

There. You are well and truly done.

Final thoughts on making this your own website

From a site meant for a career coach to a site meant exclusively for your business. You have all the tools and examples and templates waiting to serve you.

You know by now how to design a page and any section within it. You know how to design any element within any section.

You know how to edit existing template pages, sections, and elements. You also know, that if anything specific you need is not there, how to create it.

You have built the common pages that most websites have: Home, Services, About, Contact, and a Blog. If you need an extra page or two (like Products page or a Case Studies page) you know Starter Templates can get you started with a page template.

Use the pages you've already created as scaffolding. Use them to build your site by replacing the text and content within the sections of each page. Delete or add sections as you please. Build one page at a time. Within that page, build one section at a time.

Depending on the amount of content you have and the number of pages, you could complete your website in a couple of days. Even if it takes a week or more because you want to proceed slowly, it's perfectly fine.

Take your time. Experiment with elements and sections. Between Elementor and Starter Templates, there is a mind-boggling variety of choices. So taking time to discover what fits your purpose isn't a waste. It is an exciting journey toward creating something unique for your business.

Once you've got the sections ready and all the pages ready, your site is done! One of things you have to do is to let Google know you now have the real thing for it to index.

It's not Joe's site anymore. **Go to the Settings link in the back end and go through each of General, Writing, Reading, etc. sub-items. Change all details to suit your real site now.**

Especially click on **Settings > Reading**. Click the checkbox at the bottom of the page against 'Search engine visibility' to untick it. You are now ready and willing to let the search engines into your site and tell them to check it out and index it in their records.

Chapter Summary

- You learned how to optimize images for use on your website
- You created your Privacy Policy page
- You integrated your website with a third-party app Calendly
- You installed plugins for security, speed, and backups
- You tested your site for speed
- You watched the SilentMoves videos: **Video #22:** Optimize image **Video #23:** Fix appointments, **Video #24:** Wordfence for security, **Video #25:** WP-Optimize for speed, **Video #26:** UpdraftPlus for backups and **Video #27:** Test with GTMetrix

♦ ♦ ♦

11. Where to next?

Where to now?

You have solid, practical knowledge now to build your own website with WordPress and Elementor. There is always more stuff to learn, of course, but you have an adequate head start.

You have learned the skills to put together **pages** of a WordPress website. In turn, every page taught you how to handle the Elementor **sections** within them. And the sections taught you how to create and edit the Elementor **elements** (blocks or widgets) within.

You did all this with the help of the Elementor plug-in along with the Astra theme and another plugin called Starter Templates.

For some of you running active businesses, this amount of learning to get you a professional, full-featured website will feel sufficient. For others, this may only be whetting your appetite to learn more.

If you are the latter kind, here is a series of exploratory steps you may wish to take.

One, **learn more about Elementor** (free version.) Even without Starter Templates, Elementor can be your powerful ally if you use it well. I particularly recommend Elementor's own set of videos on YouTube. It is a short course of 8 videos that introduces you to the free version of

Elementor used in conjunction with their own, light-weight Hello theme (instead of Astra.)

The Hello theme performs pretty much the same function that we saw Astra do. Mainly, it helped us access and edit the header and footer regions to our satisfaction. Something that the free version of Elementor does not allow us to.

This course is accessible here: https://www.youtube.com/watch?v=icTcREd1tAg

You will receive good design suggestions as well as understand more about Elementor's start-from-scratch page design without using Starter Templates. That will help you understand the features of Elementor in depth. You will also learn about responsive websites, the ability to make your site respond and adapt itself to the device it is viewed on.

Two, you may consider **buying Elementor Pro** for its additional features. The price is under $50 (annual subscription) which is frankly nothing much considering the value you get.

Elementor Pro comes with the Theme Builder feature which lets you design everything on the site - including headers and footers, blog posts, etc. You get more freedom in designing your form or forms on the site. You receive, as you expect to, more templates and blocks you can make use of. Plus, if you're getting into building an e-commerce website, the Pro version gives you lots of integration features with WooCommerce.

Three, as the months go by, the traffic to your site will increase. You may wish to know who these visitors are, what exactly they are looking for on your website, how long they are spending on which pages and so on. You have to get **Google Analytics on your side** to help you with visitor information.

It's a free service and is integrated through one of many plugins available. It's easy to set up. At some point in the future, it is inevitable that you will need to get and understand these numbers. As usual

YouTube is your friend and you can search it for how to install Google Analytics on your WordPress site.

Four, get interested in **Search Engine Optimization**. Any business needs traffic. Understanding how to get more traffic for your website involves a good understanding of SEO. The basics are fairly simple. Learn how to get a firm grasp of the keywords at the heart of your business and how to put them to good use.

Five, the simplest to do, learn **how to update themes and plugins**. As you visit the backend of your website over time, keep an eye for those themes and plugins that require updating. WordPress will put out messages in the back end telling you what needs updating including updates to itself. Your job is to pay heed, head over to the concerned theme or plugin and click on the link that says 'update.'

This task is something you must perform diligently by checking the back end of your site at least once a week, even if you have nothing else to do there. Good maintenance can save you big trouble. Also, know that WordPress itself undergoes changes a few times in a year and will require periodic updating (very important!).

Here's wishing you years and years of a great looking website that brings you fruitful results. All the best!

◆ ◆ ◆

May I ask you for a small favor?

At the outset, I want to give you a big thanks for taking out time to read this book. You could have chosen any other book, but you took mine, and I totally appreciate this.

I hope you got at least a few actionable steps that got you started on building your own website using WordPress and Elementor. You will get better with time, rest assured.

Can I ask for 30 seconds more of your time?

I'd love it if you could leave a review about the book. Reviews may not matter to big-name authors; but they're a tremendous help for authors like me, who don't have much following. They help me to grow my readership by encouraging folks to take a chance on my books.

To put it straight– reviews are the life blood for any author.

Please leave your review on my book's Amazon page: "Design Your Own Website With WordPress." Or you can search there for the author's name: Narayan Kumar.

It will just take a few minutes of your time, but will tremendously help me to reach out to more people, so please leave your review.

Thanks for your support to my work. And I'd love to see your review.

Coming soon… Design Your Own Website With WordPress - *Volume Two*

Coming shortly! Learn all about Elementor Pro! Learn all about Elementor hosting!

Make an investment in building your business website instead of relying only on free tools. "Design Your Own Website With WordPress - VOLUME TWO" teaches you to design a more effective, professional website that gets you results. Learn advanced techniques and approaches with more SilentMoves videos showing you the key steps using **Elementor Pro**.

I'm currently writing an advanced version of Design Your Own Website with WordPress - Volume Two. It goes beyond the basics that this book covers using WordPress and Elementor free version.

The main difference of Volume Two lies in using the advanced (paid) version of Elementor. Learning to use Elementor Pro has definite advantages - greater flexibility in designing your site your way, including e-commerce sites and blog-based sites.

I'm also recommending the use of Elementor's own hosting solution instead of Bluehost. Taken together, the paid plug-in Elementor Pro along with their own hosting comes at $99 per year. It's a great bargain, in my opinion - considering the hosting is solid on a Google platform and takes care of backups as well and the Pro plugin has heaps of additional widgets.

As against a 'free' approach used in this book, Volume Two takes the approach that every business can afford a small budget to build and maintain a website.

For a small business, an annual outlay of $99 is nothing much and the benefits are huge. The power to fine-tune your content and styling is vast. Volume Two covers key aspects like:

- Setting up Elementor hosting (with your chosen domain name)
- Setting up Elementor Pro's basics
- Importing Elementor Pro's ready to use styling kits for an overall killer look for the site
- SilentMoves videos to illustrate all key steps
- Setting up your own, domain-based email using Google
- Learning a simpler workflow with just Elementor Pro (no Starter Templates as an adjunct)
- Creating professional blog designs with ease
- Designing headers and footers as well with Elementor Pro
- Accessing a larger library of widgets, pro templates and blocks for more design freedom
- Finding more features out of the box like animated headlines, slider pop-up builder, social buttons and many more
- Using the Form widget instead of a third-party plugin for a site form
- Working with custom CSS to better control the stylistic elements
- Integrating with marketing tools like MailChimp, ConvertKit, etc. for email marketing campaigns to promote your brand or business to growing body of users

– And much more!

Keep yourself updated on the release date of Volume Two here at:

www.designWPsite.com/volumetwo

About The Author

Narayan Kumar is a senio communications professional wit three decades of advertisin experience. He is a copywriter an designer who kept pace with th digital medium. As a director of h agency, he is well versed in web desig basics and build technologie including Ruby on Rails. But h favorite weapon of choice i WordPress for all the freedom it give him in design and flexibility. It also allows his clients and their teams t easily visit the admin section and make editorial changes at will withou any coding knowledge.

Narayan currently heads his WordPress consulting venture, Blu Mountain Code. Along with his wife, he consults, builds, writes, an designs anything and everything that has to do with WordPress and bran building for small business.

www.designWPsite.com is this book's website for downloads and updates

www.bluemountaincode.com is the author's business website for consulting and projects

All sample content for use along with this book can be downloaded from the author's website: www.designWPsite.com/downloads

All help videos supplementing the instructions in this book can be viewed on the author's website: www.designWPsite.com/silentmoves

Printed in Great Britain
by Amazon

23464684R00066